THE
BEST
OF THE
BRUCE
TRAIL

WINE COUNTRY TO WILDERNESS

Canadian Cataloguing in Publication Data

Jacob, Katherine, 1967 -
    The Best of the Bruce Trail: Wine Country to Wilderness

(The Conservation Lands of Ontario trail guide series; 3)
Includes bibliographical references and index.
Copyright 2000 Katherine Jacob
ISBN 13 978-0-9683425-2-7
ISBN 10 0-9683425-2-3

1. Trails - Ontario - Bruce Trail - Guidebooks. 2. Hiking - Ontario - Bruce Trail -
Guidebooks. 3. Natural Areas - Ontario - Bruce Trail - Guidebooks. 4. Bruce Trail
(Ont.) - Guidebooks. I. The Conservation Lands of Ontario (Association).
II. Title. III. Series.

FC3093.2.J32 2000   917.13   C00-931181-5
F1059.B96J32 2000

Printed in Canada.

Author: Katherine Jacob
Editor: Jim Reid
Cartography by: Paul Heersink, Paperglyphs
Front Cover Photo: Kelso Conservation Area, Rob Stimpson

Maps produced by The Conservation Lands of Ontario with permission from the:
    Bruce Trail Association, Niagara Peninsula Conservation Authority, Hamilton
    Region Conservation Authority, Conservation Halton, Credit Valley
    Conservation, Toronto and Region Conservation Authority, Nottawasaga
    Valley Conservation Authority, Grey Sauble Conservation Authority, Bruce
    Peninsula National Park, Ontario Ministry of Natural Resources, Copyright,
    © Queen's Printer, 2000, Ontario Parks

THE
BEST
OF THE
BRUCE
TRAIL

WINE COUNTRY TO WILDERNESS

Katherine Jacob

THE CONSERVATION LANDS OF ONTARIO

OTHER BOOKS BY KATHERINE JACOB

44 Country Trails
Bruce Peninsula Trails
Grand River Country Trails

This is the third trail guide published by The Conservation Lands of Ontario. The Conservation Lands are an environmental and business partnership that provides adventure and eco-tourism for visitors to watersheds managed by the following conservation authorities:

Grand River Conservation Authority
Conservation Halton
Hamilton Region Conservation Authority
Long Point Region Conservation Authority
Toronto and Region Conservation Authority

The Conservation Lands of Ontario
400 Clyde Rd., P.O. Box 729
Cambridge, Ontario
NCR 5W6
1-888-376-2212
conservationlands@grandriver.on.ca

The Conservation Lands also work in cooperation with other Conservation Authorities and groups committed to conserving and restoring our environment.

Members of Conservation Ontario

We acknowledge and thank Parks Ontario as a sponsor for the publication of *The Best of the Bruce Trail.*

This book is dedicated to my oldest brother, for wonderful childhood memories: the "stupid star," coaxing me to hold my first snake, cross-country skiing at Elora; but most of all, for calling "just because."

THANKS, ALWAYS, TO ALL MY FRIENDS AND FAMILY who provided support, valuable information and suggestions. A special thanks to all who walked these trails with me: Pete, Andrew, Joe, Barb, Blayne, Amber, Eric, Herb. Thanks to Ross and Janet McLean, Doug Sweiger, Nelson and Gene Maher, and Nathan Keeshig for introducing me to some of the trails. Thanks to Ralph Beaumont, Joan Bell, Marg Deans, Steve Bruno, Jack Wellington, Nancy White, Byron Wesson, Greg Forbes, Noel Bates, Keith Earley, Brian Tayler, Alan Foster, Barb McKean, Dave Butler, Tyler Smith, and all staff at the Conservation Authorities, Parks Canada and Ontario Parks for time, energy and assistance. Thanks to the Bruce Trail Association, Niagara Escarpment Commission and Conservancy for preserving these lands; The Bruce Trail Association and its volunteers who have built and maintained this trail, especially Ray Lowes, its founder; and Chris Walker, for hints, details and experience on the trail.

A SPECIAL THANKS TO MY EDITOR, Jim Reid, for his professional expertise and sense of humor, but most of all, for his commitment to this series; my sister for constant inspiration and support; and to Pete, for helping me on the last "leg" of this book. And a final thank you to Jaci Winters, for sharing our vision.

TABLE OF CONTENTS

Foreword

In the foreword to *Bruce Peninsula Trails*, also written by Katherine Jacob, Robert Bateman tells of his almost magnetic attraction to the Niagara Escarpment and why he chose to live there — even though he had just travelled around the world!

I met my friend Bob a way back when I first "blew in" from Saskatchewan — a refugee from the historic dust bowl of the late twenties and early thirties. I was not alone — many will remember W. O. Mitchell, Max & Dennis Braithwaite, Elwood Glover and John Diefenbaker, all with indomitable spirit and resourcefulness born of humble prairie roots. Like the prairie gopher and the tumbleweed, we were all survivors.

At Hamilton I missed the 'freedom to ramble' that was part of prairie life but soon became involved in field trips organized by the Hamilton Naturalists' Club, the Federation of Ontario Naturalists, and the Sierra Club. While immersed in this fertile milieu, I put forward the idea of a nature trail that would follow the wild and rocky spine of the Niagara Escarpment from Queenston to Tobermory.

In those early days, 1959, 1960,...1967 it seemed that we had a tiger by the tail! A Bruce Trail Committee soon became the Bruce Trail Association. A head-quarters for the BTA was found in collaboration with the Royal Botanical Gardens at a beautiful location, "Rasberry House."

Since the Honorable René Brunelle officiated at the grand opening of the Trail as a Centennial project in 1967, at Tobermory, I have continued to be involved: Secretary, Honorary President, and by serving for ten years on the Niagara Escarpment Commission.

There is a challenge and a joy in trying to establish a closer relationship with nature. My early 'freedom to ramble' has been replaced by safe trails. For your mental and physical health, I urge you to go for a walk. Extend your feel for this wonderful land through the soles of your feet. Read this book, which I am happy to recommend as a delightful companion to the famous BTA Reference Guide.

Go for it!! You will end up thanking everyone who urged you to take this path.

Ray Lowes, Bruce Trail Founder.

INTRODUCTION

After years of hiking the Bruce Trail, why do I return? For its ever changing vistas each season, the lure of an ancient landscape, the wind that dances through old-growth forests.

The Niagara Escarpment is ancient tropical oceans, fossils older than dinosaurs, and sea caves abandoned by glaciers. It's a UNESCO World Biosphere Reserve and one of the few undeveloped areas in the most densely populated region of Canada. To intimately know such a large landform, you have to hike it. Feel each step. Explore each lookout. This is the Bruce Trail.

Running through southern Ontario, the Bruce Trail is Canada's oldest footpath, opened in 1967 as the Centennial Trail. It's also one of the longest trails, holding onto the coattails of a very big brother, the Niagara Escarpment. Being the grand daddy of trails, it serves as a major link for other trail systems, such as the Trans Canada Trail, the Caledon Trailway, and the Cambridge to Hamilton Rail Trail.

Connecting conservation areas, provincial parks and nature reserves in one continuous pathway, the Bruce Trail is the string between these pearls. You'll see many faces of Ontario, from 30 metre high limestone cliffs, windswept old-growth cedars and cobblestone beaches to dense forests, hidden waterfalls, and pastoral farmland. You'll walk over a variety of terrain, from glacial river valleys and limestone ridges with secret caves to county roads and railroad tracks. And, you'll experience the last remaining areas of wilderness left in this region of Ontario.

The Bruce Trail was the dream of one man, Ray Lowes. Built and maintained by volunteers, the Bruce Trail started out in his Hamilton living room, where local children licked stamps and envelopes to mail "The Bruce Trail News." Trail headquarters remained at Ray's home for a long time before relocating to the Rasberry House in the Royal Botanical Gardens in Hamilton.

The Bruce Trail is a partnership with a number of organizations. Conservation authorities and provincial parks that allow passage on their properties (the Niagara Escarpment Parks and Open Space System.). Private landowners that grant the same privilege. Volunteers (Bruce Trail Association members) who build and maintain the trail. It's the volunteers who are the strength of this organization. Even in conservation areas and on city property, the trail is maintained by volunteers. I would encourage you to become a member and support this organization (see the Bruce Trail page).

The Best of the Bruce Trail is an introduction to this long-distance pathway, featuring scenic sections that are easily accessible and short enough for a day hike. To get more detailed information on every section of the trail and topographical maps, buy The Bruce Trail Reference. It also supports trail maintenance and further land purchase to secure the trail in perpetuity.

The Bruce Trail makes the Niagara Escarpment accessible, one of the few World Biosphere Reserves on the planet that people can afford to visit. There is no hiking fee, no tour guide required, just a request that you respect the trail and its beauty.

It's my hope that when you've completed this book, you'll be inspired to walk the entire Bruce Trail, from Niagara to Tobermory. You'll join hundreds of Bruce Trail Association Members who have hiked the trail from beginning to end. Some make it a journey of years, heading out each weekend to complete a different section. Others take a vacation to hike a large section and camp overnight at designated spots.

It is also my hope that as you hike this trail, you will start caring about and valuing the Niagara Escarpment. That you will oppose development and escarpment annexations that will adversely affect its habitat, and, even threaten its World Biosphere Reserve status.

We who hike in the natural world, go freely when we need to escape, to explore, to breathe fresh air. But we must relate to nature in more ways. We must be caretakers, stewards of our pathways, and, our earth.

The Bruce Trail drew attention to the Niagara Escarpment and it was designated a UNESCO World Biosphere Reserve in 1991. Yet this natural area is still threatened with mining and development for homes and resorts. If you want the pleasure of the escarpment, walk along the Bruce Trail. If you want your children to experience this World Biosphere Reserve, help secure the trail and parks along the Escarpment by becoming a member of the Bruce Trail Association . . . so you can return year after year, for the ever changing vistas and the wind dancing through the trees.

Enjoy the Trails!

Katherine

THE BRUCE TRAIL

Every year more than 400,000 people visit the Niagara Escarpment World Biosphere Reserve via the Bruce Trail. They have the Bruce Trail Association (BTA) to thank.

The BTA is a volunteer based charitable organization with 8,000 members. Its mandate is to secure, develop and manage a public footpath along the Escarpment, thereby promoting and preserving the natural and cultural integrity of the Niagara Escarpment World Biosphere Reserve and its 300 species of birds, 53 different mammals, 35 reptiles and amphibians, 90 kinds of fish and rare thousand year old eastern white cedars and native orchids.

Bruce Trail founders were naturalists who envisioned the Bruce Trail as an ecological corridor linking other green spaces along the Escarpment. Since its opening in 1967 as Canada's Centennial Trail, hundreds of volunteers have contributed more than 100,000 hours of volunteer work per year to develop and maintain the 800 km (500 mi) Bruce Trail and over 290 km (180 mi) of side trails. They are the lifeblood of this trail.

Six million Ontarians live within a ninety minute drive of the Bruce Trail. You too can become a link in this preservation chain. The annual membership fee of $40 includes membership in the Bruce Trail Association and one of its nine clubs, a club newsletter and the BTA quarterly magazine, the *Bruce Trail News,* plus special member discounts for products and services. Visit the Bruce Trail website for more information, to join on line or to make a donation on their secure site.

The Bruce Trail Association
PO Box 857
Hamilton, Ontario
L8N 3N9

Telephone 905-529-6821, 1-800-665-4453
Fax 905-529-6823
e-mail: info@brucetrail.org, www.brucetrail.org

How To Use This Guide

This guide offers brief descriptions and detailed maps for each trail. At the start of each description, the distance is mentioned. A loop trail means a return to the starting point via another route. If linear, the trail returns to the starting point via the same route. Some trails have parking lots at beginning and end points and other access locations allowing for you to arrange a car shuttle. Please pay close attention to parking areas. *The trail crosses many private lands and the generosity of private owners can be reversed if this privilege is not respected by following The Bruce Trail Users' Code.*

Many areas have other trails on their properties and some of these trails connect with the Bruce trail. These are listed in brackets as "Other Area Trails." The Bruce Trail also connects with major trail links such as the Caledon Trailway and Ganaraska Trail. Other trails are close to one another and can easily be combined into a day or weekend trip.

Major trail links are briefly described and highlighted on the large, fold-out map, but consult individual trail guides for detailed information (addresses and phone numbers are provided).

In the upfront trail information, you'll see an entry marked as "BTG". This refers to where the featured section appears in The Bruce Trail Reference. If you want to walk a longer section of the trail or further explore the Bruce Trail, please buy this guide. It has detailed descriptions and topographical maps for the entire trail.

Trails are marked in various ways depending on the area. The Bruce Trail marking system follows painted white blazes on trees, rocks and poles. A single blaze means that the trail continues in the same direction. Two blazes placed one above the other indicate a change of direction. If the top blaze is offset, this indicates the direction of the turn. A blue blaze indicates a side trail. You must pay careful attention to blazes. If there are few trees or fences, the blazes will be sparse and may even appear on rocks. In the summer blazes can be hidden by dense vegetation. Also watch for arrows indicating a sudden change in direction.

Symbols for trail features and facilities appear on the Individual Trail Maps. The matrix in the back section (Trail Features At A Glance) lists permitted uses. Some areas offer trackset skiing, but snowshoes can be used in winter on most walking trails. The special features listing indicates unique trail information such as special events and interpretive centres. It also indicates other seasonal conservation area and trail uses, such as snowmobiling and hunting. If a conservation area allows hunting, call before visiting in the spring and fall and make sure you wear a safety vest or brightly coloured clothing, or you can visit the area outside of the hunting season.

A phone number for more information on a specific trail is listed, only if it differs from the conservation authority or land management agency's main telephone number. Please call during the off season to ensure the area is open. If it is closed, hiking is often permitted, but facilities won't be available.

Many of the trails in this book are rugged and it's best to hike with another person. Be sure to let someone know of your plans and your expected return time. Be careful when walking along cobble beaches as loose rocks can easily twist an ankle. When rock scrambling, make sure you have a solid hand and foothold. If rocks are wet, they can be slippery.

If rock scrambling, especially in coniferous forests, be careful where you put your feet and hands. Trails in the Bruce Peninsula are one of the last sanctuaries for the eastern Massasauga rattle snake. If you hear a snake's rattler, locate it visually and move carefully around it. Snakes aren't aggressive and will not chase you. The Massasauga is on the endangered species list and is seldom seen. You should also be cautious around black bears. Most of the time wild animals are more scared of you and will run away. Never feed a wild animal, corner it, or get between a mother and its young. If you have an unexpected encounter with a bear, never turn your back and run. It might trigger a predatory response. Rather make loud noises (shout, yell, whistle, clap) and raise your hands, to leave no doubt in the bear's mind that you are a human and not an animal. Then back away slowly. If a bear follows you, put your pack down slowly, to distract the bear while you retreat.

Environmental Ethics

Since these trails are primarily for the enjoyment of nature, there are environmental ethics to observe. Widening a trail by foot can alter the habitat and some plants take years to grow back. Consequently, proceed directly through wet, muddy spots. Don't litter, or trample vegetation around the edges of a trail. And don't deliberately make noise to spook animals; they need their energy to search for food.

As adventurous as they may look, creating side trails should be avoided as vegetation may be harmed. Stay on marked trails and within lookout area boundaries to help protect the rare plants and fragile natural resources, as well as for your own safety.

Pets must be kept on a leash at all times. Dogs can chase wildlife, harm ground-nesting songbirds, and transfer poison ivy to owners.

Safety Notes

On a cautionary note, there are inherent risks in travelling on foot through natural areas. On escarpment properties, many trails follow the escarpment edge and there aren't fences to guard against steep slopes. Some crevices, starting right at the edge of the trail, are hidden by pine trees and bushes. Depending on weather and time of the year, some trail surfaces near the water can be muddy or icy. Limestone can also be dangerous and slippery when wet.

Poison ivy takes many forms and is quite rampant off the maintained trail areas. Look for three shiny leaflets on a single stem with the middle leaf having a longer stalk.

Some trails are in remote locations. Lock all valuables in the trunk of your car to ensure the safety of your belongings.

The Bruce Trail Users' Code

Hike only along marked routes, especially on farmland, do not take short cuts.

Do not climb fences - use the stiles.

Respect the privacy of people living along the trail.

Leave the trail cleaner than you found it, carry out all litter.

Light cooking fires at official campsites only, drench fires after use (better still, carry a lightweight stove).

Leave flowers and plants for others to enjoy.

Do not damage live trees or strip off bark.

Keep dogs on a leash, especially on or near farmland.

Protect and do not disturb wildlife.

Leave only your thanks and take nothing but photographs.

Trail Etiquette

Unless otherwise indicated, the Bruce Trail is strictly for walkers. Some links with the Bruce Trail, such as the Trans Canada Trail and Caledon Trailway are multi-use. Multi-use trails, may be shared by hikers, mountain bikers, equestrians and joggers. Here are some trail etiquette guidelines for multi-use systems:

- Stay to the right and allow other users room to pass on your left. For example, joggers and cyclists should avoid travelling in 'packs.'

- Yield to pedestrians; they have the right of way on multi-use trails.

- When passing others, sound your bell (if on a bike) or call out ("On your left") and then pass safely on the user's left side. Be especially cautious when approaching horseback riders, children, or dogs from behind.

- Say "Hi" when passing or approaching horseback riders, especially when on a bike. Horses have a large peripheral vision and may not perceive you as a human when you're on a bicycle. They are nervous animals and their first instinct will be to run. When approaching horseback riders, let them pass unless the rider indicates otherwise. If approaching from behind, slow to their speed and from 15 metres (49 feet) away ask if it is safe to pass slowly.

- Ride slowly down hills, under and across bridges and where trails curve sharply. Reduce your speed when the trail is busy or when your visibility is limited.

- Watch for surface hazards like broken glass, gravel and potholes. When cycling, cross railway tracks at a right angle to avoid getting your front wheel caught.

- Don't snowshoe over groomed ski trails. It breaks up the tracks for skiers.

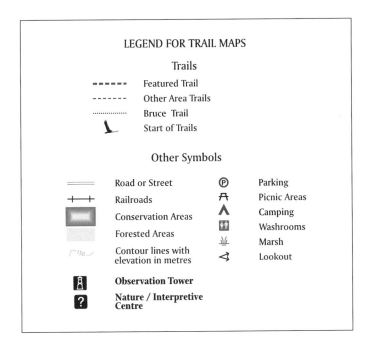

LEGEND FOR TRAIL MAPS

Trails

- - - - - - Featured Trail

- - - - - - Other Area Trails

.... Bruce Trail

⌐ Start of Trails

Other Symbols

═══ Road or Street		℗	Parking
┼─┼ Railroads		⊼	Picnic Areas
▭ Conservation Areas		Λ	Camping
Forested Areas		⚏	Washrooms
⌐150⌐ Contour lines with elevation in metres		⚲	Marsh
		◁	Lookout
Observation Tower			
Nature / Interpretive Centre			

Trans Canada Trail

Ontario trails make up about 25% of the total length of the 15,000 kilometre (9,320 mile) Trans Canada Trail (TCT), Canada's coast-to-coast trail system. The 11 kilometre (6.8 mile) Caledon Trail Link, for example, connects Inglewood on the Caledon Trailway to the Forks of the Credit Provincial Park on the Elora Cataract Trailway. The Hamilton to Brantford Rail Trail and the Cambridge to Paris Rail Trail are also major connecting links in this trail system.

Trans Canada Trail Foundation
43 Westminster Ave. N.
Montreal West, Quebec
H4X 1Y8
(800) 465-3636
e-mail: info@tctrail.ca
website: www.tctrail.ca

Ontario Trails Council
Box 462, Stn. D.
Etobicoke, Ontario
M9A 4X4

The Ganaraska Trail

The Ganaraska Trail runs for 500 km from Lake Ontario to Georgian Bay covering a variety of terrain: shoreline, rugged Canadian Shield, rolling hills, drumlin fields, and sand dunes. It also leads through the Kawartha Lakes, skirts the Minnesing Swamp and a side trail ends up at the Wye Marsh Center. Only experienced hikers should attempt the Wilderness Section, where the land is rugged and trail markers sometimes take the form of rock cairns.

Ganaraska Hiking Trail Association
Box 693 Orillia, Ontario L3V 6K7

Other Bests

In previous books I've written, I've mentioned other Bruce Trail sections that are also deserving of a "best" status. So this book wouldn't be repetitive of my others, I didn't include previously mentioned trails in *The Best of the Bruce Trail*, but I'd like to draw your attention to those I also consider the "Best Of":

44 COUNTRY TRAILS
Crawford Lake Trails
Mount Nemo Trails
Rattlesnake Point Trails
Dundas Valley Trails
Royal Botanical Gardens
North Shore Trail
Ball's Falls Trail
Woodend Silurian Adventure Trail

BRUCE PENINSULA TRAILS
Georgian Bay-Marr Lake Trail
Halfway Log Dump Trail
Devil's Monument Trail
Lion's Head Trail
Barrow Bay Loop
Jack Poste-Hope Bay Trail
Cape Croker Trail
Spirit Rock Trail
Inglis Falls Trail
Old Baldy Trail

HOG BACK SIDE TRAIL

LOCATION:	Short Hills Provincial Park, Pelham
DISTANCE:	2.3 km (1.4 mile) linear
RATING:	Beginner
BTG:	Niagara, map #3, S. 38.6-40.2
HIGHLIGHT:	Favourite of Ray Lowes, founder of The Bruce Trail

TRAIL SURFACE: Hard packed earth, rocks, grass

DIRECTIONS: From the QEW Niagara, take Hwy. 406 south toward Welland. Turn right on Glendale Ave. (89) and left on DeCew Rd. When you reach DeCew and Cataract Rd., Morningstar Grist Mill is 0.5 km on the left hand side.

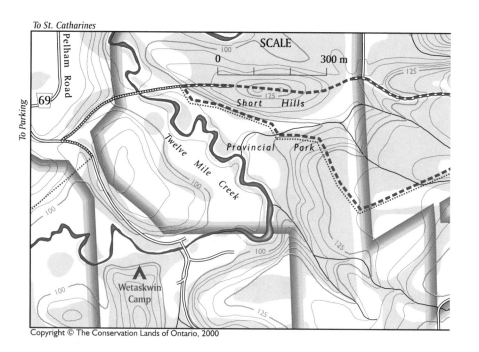

There's an intimate feeling on this trail, where hills fold into one another and the winding path opens to every switchback. If you visit early in the morning, you'll see deer running up these hills and descending into the next valley, seemingly out of nowhere, which, is how you may feel the moment you leave the hydro lines and winding road behind. The hills envelop you.

On this trail, your view is drawn downward as much as over the hills. In the valley bottom, the creek widens along the base of hills and branches through the ravines. After crossing the bridge, you can head up to the Wetaskiwin Scout Camp or finish the loop that continues for a short while, along sharp turns on DeCew Rd.

This trail returns to Morningstar Mills Museum. This century old building once contained three separate mills. Later a sawmill, carpentry and blacksmith shop, cidermill and shoddy mill were added. If you walk into the museum, you'll be transported from the hills to history. The museum houses old pictures and turn of the century machinery, among them millstacks, a double roller mill and bucket elevators.

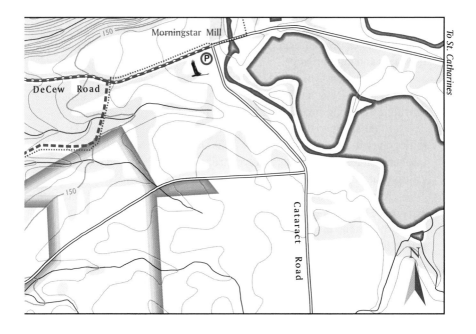

ROCKWAY FALLS SIDE TRAIL

LOCATION:	Rockway Conservation Area, Vineland
DISTANCE:	2.6 km (1.6 mile) loop
RATING:	Intermediate
BTG:	Niagara, map #3, S. 46.3-47.0
HIGHLIGHT:	Waterfall

TRAIL SURFACE: Hard packed earth, rocks, grass

DIRECTIONS:　From the QEW Niagara, take exit 57 at Victoria Avenue (Regional Road 24). Travel south and turn left on Regional Road 669. After crossing 9th Ave., you'll see the Community Centre on your left.

During the last Ice Age a huge glacier carved a U-shaped valley into the Escarpment. This trail follows the large ravine. In the spring, Fifteen-Mile Creek plunges 40 metres (131 feet) over the Escarpment edge, feeding a forest floor covered in wildflowers. Before proceeding on The Bruce Trail, stop at the Rockway Community Centre where a scenic lookout peers onto these falls and into the gorge.

From the start you'll see large boulders, ones that tumbled down from the escarpment. Now covered with moss, they collect dust and spores, providing a growing environment for larger plants.

In the summer, the trail descends into the creek valley blanketed with thick grapevines and lined with sweet fruits of wild strawberry and raspberry. It follows the creek and eventually crosses it to ascend the escarpment.

Before traversing this waterway, take a small trail to your right and explore the former Louth salt springs. They were used in the late 1700s and during the War of 1812 when salt was scarce. Now it's a scenic outcrop, perfect for a lunch break. The trail loops back on Pelham Rd.

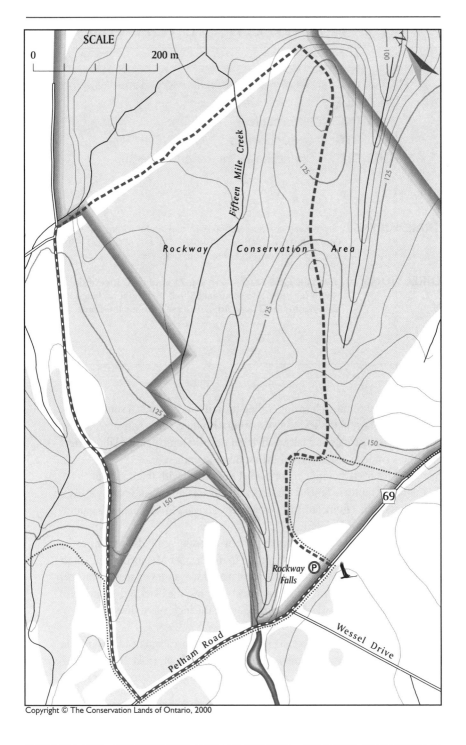

SCALE

0   200 m

Fifteen Mile Creek

Rockway   Conservation   Area

100

125

125

125

125

150

150

150

69

Rockway
Falls   P

Pelham Road

Wessel Drive

BEAMER TRAIL

LOCATION:	Beamer Memorial Conservation Area, Grimsby
DISTANCE:	1.6 km (1 mile) loop
RATING:	Intermediate
BTG:	Iroquoia, map #5, S. 0.9-2.4
HIGHLIGHT:	Spring hawk migration, waterfall

TRAIL SURFACE: From Beamer Conservation Area parking lot to the first lookout is stone dust (wheelchair accessible). The rest of the trail is hard packed earth with tree roots and rocks.

DIRECTIONS: From the QEW Niagara take exit 71 at Christie Street Exit. Travel south (changes into Mountain Road), turn right on Ridge Rd. W. and right onto Quarrie Rd. You'll see signs for the Conservation Area.

They come each spring, riding the tail winds of warm southerly breezes. They fill the sky: eagles soaring with their wings spread wide, hawks circling in thermals and falcons flying quickly in long, pointed silhouettes. Others come to watch them: birders, hikers, families.

It's overwhelming to look up at a sky filled with thousands of migrating raptors. Since it borders wide open lakes, offers strong air currents, and a funnel of safe passage, the Niagara Escarpment is a guiding landmark during migration.

Each year these raptors fly to their breeding grounds further north, and hikers make an annual migration to the Beamer Memorial Trail. In the wide open field at the start of this trail, you'll see kettles of soaring raptors: the many tail bands of the red-shouldered hawk, the black wrist patches of the rough-legged hawk, and if you're lucky, the high speed dive of a peregrine.

From this field you can enter the forested area and head towards the lookouts along the escarpment edge. At each lookout, make sure you gaze overhead as well. The scenery in the springtime is more spectacular in the sky.

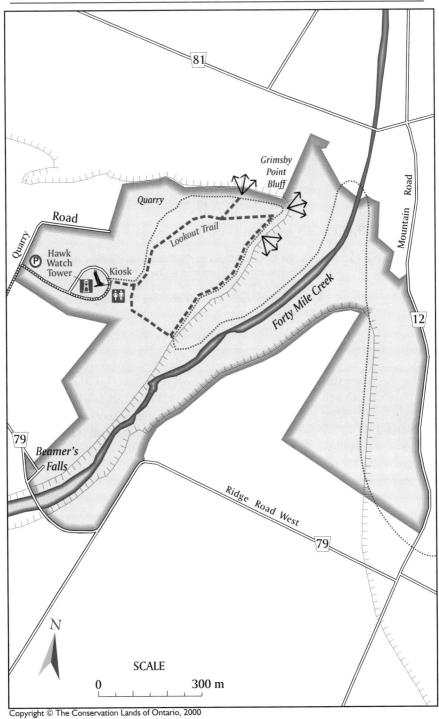

81

Grimsby
Point
Bluff

Quarry

Road

Lookout Trail

Quarry

Mountain Road

Hawk
Watch
Tower

P

Kiosk

Forty Mile Creek

12

79

Beamer's
Falls

Ridge Road West

79

N

SCALE

0   300 m

DEVIL'S PUNCH BOWL TRAIL

LOCATION:	Devil's Punch Bowl Conservation Area, Stoney Creek
DISTANCE:	2.2 km (1.4 mile) loop
RATING:	Intermediate
BTG:	Iroquoia, map #6, S. 20.4-21.1
HIGHLIGHT:	One of the largest and most complete vertical natural exposures of Silurian stratified rock along the escarpment, waterfall

TRAIL SURFACE: Grass, hard packed earth, rocks and a bit of pavement

DIRECTIONS: From the Toronto/Hamilton QEW Niagara take the Centennial Parkway/Hwy. 20 exit and turn south. Climb the escarpment and turn left on Green Mountain Rd. (first traffic light) and immediate left on First Rd. East. Turn left on Ridge Rd. The parking lot is on your right.

Stoney Creek tumbles for twenty metres (66 feet) over the rim of the Devil's Punch Bowl, a one hundred metre wide (328 foot) rock face that exposes 40 million years of geological history. From the lookout near the parking lot, follow the side trail, indicated by the blue markers, that leads down steep valley walls into the creek bottom. Turn left through the forest and walk a short while along the railway line before taking a rocky pathway that leads to the punch bowl.

From this perspective you'll see layers of coloured stone, sand and fossils deposited by ancient seas. It's a unique opportunity to view one of the largest and most complete vertical natural exposures of Silurian stratified rock along the escarpment. From Queenston Formation red shale and Lockport Formation chert beds, you'll also see the most southerly exposures of Cabot Head (grey shale) and Manitoulin (shale dolomite) formations.

Before following the trail on the opposite creekbank, cross over the railroad tracks and follow the blue side trail markers along the creek and into Battlefield Park, site of the 1813 Battle of Stoney Creek. You can visit the Gage Homestead, now a museum and climb the tower for a view of the CN Tower and Lake Ontario. The Bruce Trail loops through red oak and white pine forest and returns for 500 metres (1640 feet) along the road.

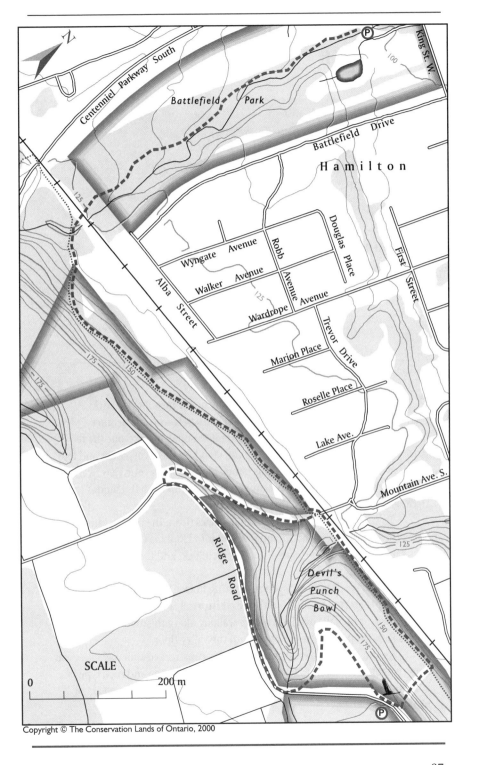

Copyright © The Conservation Lands of Ontario, 2000

ROCK CHAPEL /
BORER'S FALLS TRAIL

LOCATION: Borer's Falls Conservation Area, Flamborough
DISTANCE: 2.5 km (1.6 mile) linear
RATING: Intermediate
BTG: Iroquoia, map #8, S. 67.7 - 65.2
HIGHLIGHT: Waterfall, geology exhibit

TRAIL SURFACE: Grass, hard packed earth, rocks and a bit of pavement

DIRECTIONS: From Hwy. 401, take Hwy. 6 South. Turn right on York Rd. After passing Hwy. 5, park at the pump station on your right-hand side. From Hwy. 403, take Hwy. 6 north, turn left on York Rd. and park at the pump station.

From bobolinks and butterflies in the upper meadow to hawks migrating along the escarpment edge, Rock Chapel has three distinct habitats: an upper plateau, cliff face, and talus slope. It's also one the few places in southern Ontario where you can stand on the escarpment and look across at another section of it. This bench lookout takes your view over the west end of Coote's Paradise, downtown Hamilton to the left, Dundas to the right, and the escarpment across from you.

To start on this trail, find the blue blazes (from the pump station) along the edge of the meadow and descend into Hopkins Creek Valley. You'll pass rare sedges, and an isolated stand of hemlock, and then walk up the escarpment talus slope.

As you reach the road, you're entering Rock Chapel, named for a frame chapel erected in 1822 (you'll see a historical society plaque along the road). Stop at the falls overlook before walking along the road. You'll see Borers Falls drop 25 metres (82 feet) into the valley floor.

As you round the escarpment, a newly constructed stairway takes you along a geological exhibit. Each exposed formation name and rock type is labeled. In an escarpment minute you walk through 420 million years of history.

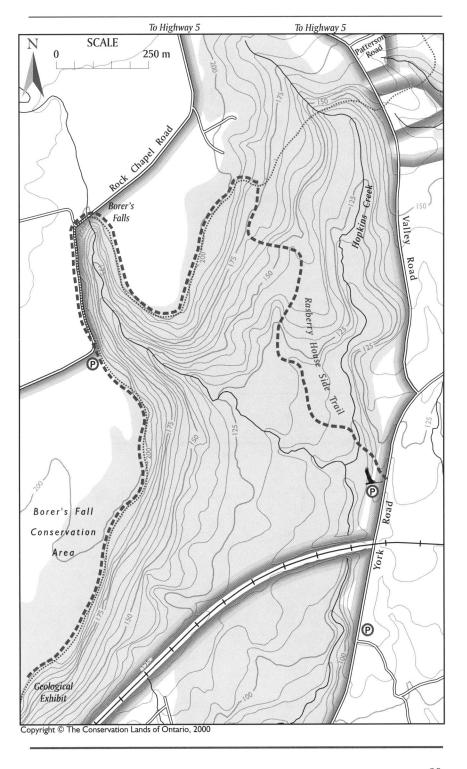

N

SCALE

0   250 m

Patterson Road

Rock Chapel Road

Borer's Falls

Hopkins Creek

Valley Road

Rasberry House Side Trail

P

Borer's Fall
Conservation
Area

P

York Road

P

Geological
Exhibit

TIFFANY FALLS TRAIL

LOCATION: Dundas Valley Conservation Area, Ancaster
DISTANCE: 5.7 km (3.5 mile) linear
[Other area trails: 40 km (25 mile) trail network. Please refer to the Dundas Valley Trail Map]
RATING: Intermediate
BTG: Iroquoia, map #8, S. 46.1-51.8
HIGHLIGHT: Waterfalls, Carolinian forest, Hermitage ruins
LINK: Hamilton-to-Cambridge Rail Trail

TRAIL SURFACE: Grass, hard packed earth, rocks and a bit of pavement

DIRECTIONS: From 403, take Mohawk Rd. W. and turn left on Wilson St./Hwy. 2. Turn right onto Sulphur Springs Rd. and turn right at the next stop sign. Follow this winding road for 1.5 km. Park at the Hermitage Ruins on your right.

MORE INFORMATION:
Trail Centre (905) 627-1233. For trail conditions check www.hamrca.on.ca or call 905-627-1233. Admission fee applies.

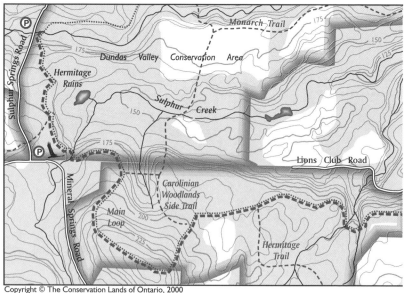

Copyright © The Conservation Lands of Ontario, 2000

This is a great trail to visit in the rain. You can sit under the many rock overhangs and stare deep into the forest, the misty air blending the leaves into one large green tree. From this dry vantage point, you can hear the rain drop on leaves and then fall onto ones lower in the valley.

Any walk through Dundas Valley offers this kind of discovery. There are historical ruins, rare Carolinian forests and rock overlooks that jut out over the steep valley walls.

As this trail leaves the conservation area near Old Ancaster Road, you enter typical Bruce Trail terrain: rocks to step over, steep descents and the hidden waterfalls. Sherman Falls first appears at an 11.5 metre (38 foot) drop where Ancaster Creek flows over the escarpment. This waterfall, fed by springs from its headwaters, has a strong, continuous flow.

Continue through the scenic ravine in the Tiffany Creek valley until you cross Wilson St. Tiffany Creek tumbles 6.5 metres from a broad valley above the escarpment into a V-shaped ravine below. A short side trail leads you to the waterfall. It's a rough walk, crossing talus slope with steep, narrow sections.

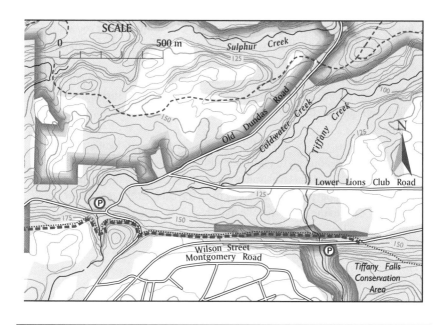

STAIRWAY TO SPENCER GORGE TRAIL

LOCATION:	Spencer Gorge Wilderness Area, Dundas
DISTANCE:	6 km (3.7 mile) linear
RATING:	Intermediate and advanced
BTG:	Iroquoia, map #8, S. 57.4 - 61.1
HIGHLIGHT:	Waterfalls
LINK:	Bruce Trail

TRAIL SURFACE: Hard packed earth with tree roots and rocks

DIRECTIONS: To reach Webster's Falls parking lot take Hwy. 8 from Dundas. Turn right on Brock Road and right at the flashing light onto Harvest Rd. Turn right onto Short Road and left onto Fallsview Rd and follow the signs for the parking lot.

Few people take the secret route to Spencer Gorge. The Bruce trail follows the creek as it meanders through the valley, tumbles over rocks and pushes past fallen logs. It traces the creek as it rounds a bend and broadens at the base of Webster Falls.

Most people view this waterfall from the top of the escarpment. They miss the intimate approach the Bruce Trail offers. Walking through the valley, you can stop to sit on a giant boulder and watch leaves flow through the rapids.

At the base of Webster's Falls, look up at the escarpment and see the cliffs you'll be walking on to reach Tew's Falls and Dundas Peak. When you're ready to leave the creek valley, be careful walking up the stairs. The stone can be slippery with water spray from the falls. At the top, follow the trail as it leads to the 41 metre (134 foot) high Tews Falls, a waterfall once as large as the 52 metre (170 foot) high Horseshoe Falls in Niagara.

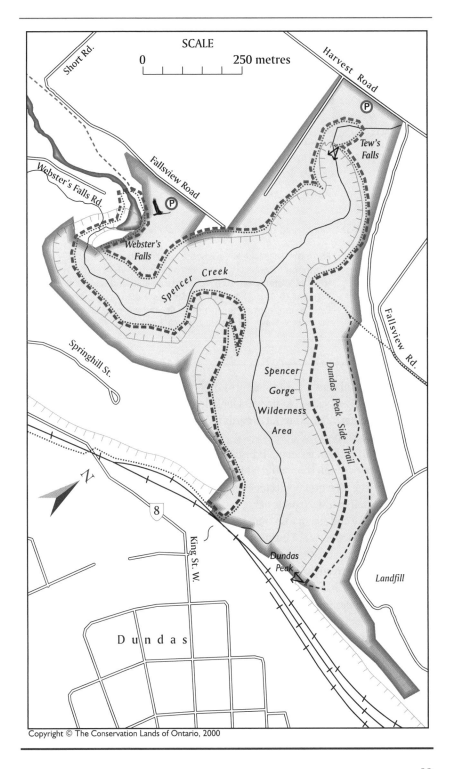

SCALE

0   250 metres

Short Rd.

Harvest Road

Ⓟ

Tew's Falls

Fallsview Road

Webster's Falls Rd.

Ⓟ

Webster's Falls

Spencer Creek

Fallsview Rd.

Springhill St.

Spencer Gorge Wilderness Area

Dundas Peak Side Trail

N

8

King St. W.

Dundas Peak

Landfill

D u n d a s

W A T E R D O W N   T R A I L

LOCATION:	Waterdown
DISTANCE:	3.6 km (2.2 mile) linear
RATING:	Beginner
BTG:	Iroquoia, map #9, S. 72.9 - 76.5
HIGHLIGHT:	Smokey Hollow Gorge, deep ravines

TRAIL SURFACE: Grass, hard packed earth, rocks and a bit of pavement

DIRECTIONS: From the 401, take Hwy. 6 south towards Hamilton. At Clappison's Corners, turn left onto Hwy. 5. When you enter the town of Waterdown, turn right onto Mill St. and park at the waterfall (0.6 km/0.4 mi to the Smokey Hollow pkg). For Snake Rd. Parking, turn right onto Main St. and left onto Snake Rd. (Main St. ends at Snake Rd.) It's 1.2 km (0.7 mi) from Snake Rd to the parking lot.

This trail winds, twists and turns over ravines as it descends into the Grindstone Creek valley. At first you look deeply into the ravines, from one ridge to another. Then your focus turns to the creek, its branches jutting along the valley bottom.

This trail is movement. It begins in the forest and leads toward the falls. Halfway through, as you start to follow the creek, the landscape changes. The even ground becomes rugged with boulders jutting into the hills. The stairs on steep parts help you ascend to Smokey Hollow.

Smoke and steam rose from the Grindstone Creek valley in the 1800s and Smokey Hollow was a busy milling area. It's difficult to imagine that this quiet valley was a bustling industrial centre. Many chimneys dispatched smoke and steam and the valley earned the name Smokey Hollow. By early 1900s, as steam and electricity replaced water power, mill operators had to contend with declining markets and more efficient energy sources. Fire claimed several of the mills and the final blow came in 1912 when a railway was constructed through the valley. A placard at the waterfall lookout displays a picture of railway construction in 1912, and, the industry that was around it.

More spectacular than the scene at this overlook is the hidden waterfall that cascades down a distant hillside along the trail. Don't miss it!

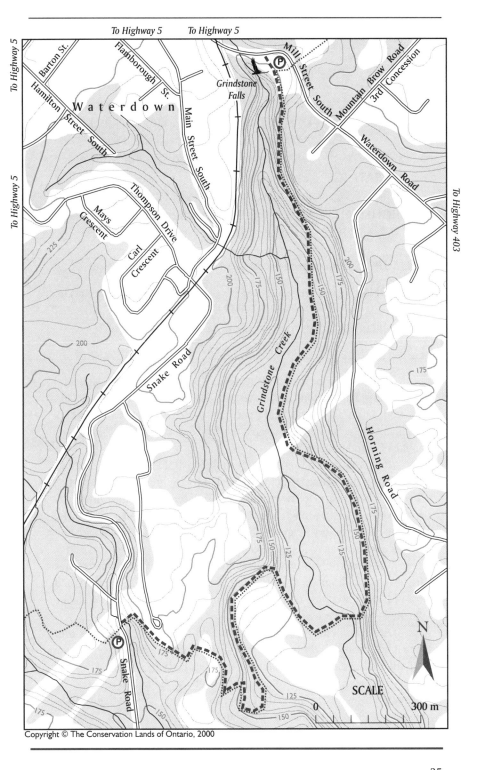

NASSAGAWEYA CANYON TRAIL

LOCATION:	Crawford Lake Conservation Area, Milton
DISTANCE:	3.9 km (2.4 mile) loop (Other area trails: 1.4 km/0.9 mile Crawford Lake, 1.7 km/1 mile Woodland, 2 km/1.2 mile Pine Ridge, 2.6 km/1.6 mile Escarpment Trail loop)
RATING:	Intermediate
BTG:	Iroquoia, map #11, S. 112.3-115.7
HIGHLIGHT:	Meromictic lake, old farm foundation walls
LINK:	Crawford Lake trails

TRAIL SURFACE: Grass, hard packed earth, rocks and a bit of pavement

DIRECTIONS: From Hwy. 401, take the Guelph Line south exit (Exit 312) to Steeles Ave., turn east to the park entrance.

MORE INFORMATION: (905) 854-0234. Admission fee applies.

Think about the insurmountable odds of settling Escarpment land, with its large boulders and uneven terrain. Then, visit Crawford Lake. On this trail you'll walk along an old stone wall covered with moss and plants, a testament to the families that cleared this land and moved these huge boulders, without machinery.

Surprises stretch from the large to the small along this trail. After the lookout over the Nassagaweya Canyon, you leave the groomed Conservation Area trails behind and follow typical Bruce Trail terrain into the canyon. It's on the steep descent, while you're stepping between, over and around rocks, that you have to keep your eye on the moist ground. This is ideal salamander habitat and you may be fortunate enough to see the fluid movements of these little contortionists on the forest floor. Many salamanders in this area are rare, and their numbers are reduced from the depletion of wetlands and loss of habitat, so please don't disturb them. They are an important link in the fragile wetland ecosystem.

After this point you reach a flat, straight section with many logs, ideal for a lunch break. As the trail rises out of the valley, the view stretches across to Rattlesnake Point and down toward the creek bed where you just walked.

The Leech Porter side trail leads through a meadow and a pine plantation before returning to the Conservation Area. It's here that you'll see the stone wall, an old farm foundation and former apple orchard. Stop at the rare meromictic Crawford Lake on your return.

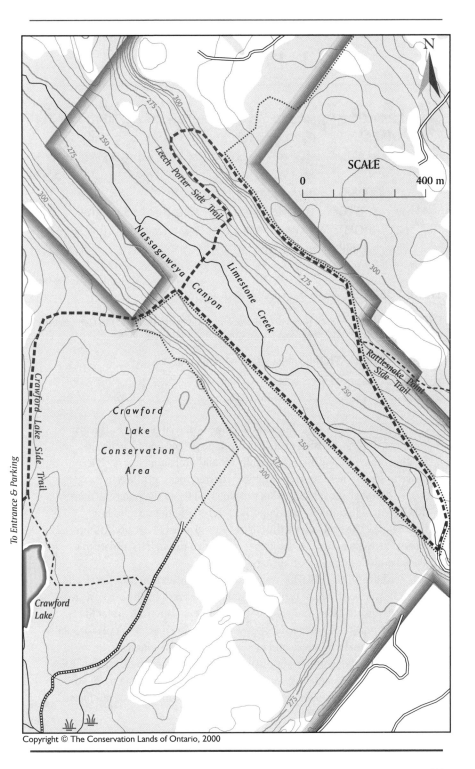

N

SCALE

0   400 m

Leech Porter Side Trail

Nassagaweya Canyon

Limestone Creek

Rattlesnake Point Side Trail

To Entrance & Parking

Crawford Lake Side Trail

Crawford Lake Conservation Area

Crawford Lake

SIXTEEN MILE CREEK TRAIL

LOCATION:	Hilton Falls Conservation Area, Milton
DISTANCE:	6 km (3.7 mile) linear (Other area trails: 2 km (1.2 mile) Red Oak, 4 km (2.5 miles) Hilton Falls, 9.5 km (6 miles) Beaver Dam Trail loops)
RATING:	Beginner to intermediate
BTG:	Toronto, map #11, Hilton Falls Side Trail, S. 1.8
HIGHLIGHT:	Sixteen Mile Creek, Waterfall, mill ruins
LINK:	Bruce Trail

TRAIL SURFACE: Gravel, hard packed earth and rocks

DIRECTIONS: From Hwy. 401 take Guelph Line North (exit 312) to Campbellville Rd., turn east to the Conservation Area entrance.

MORE INFORMATION: (905) 854-0262. Admission fee applies.

Sixteen Mile Creek flows through one of the largest forest tracts in southern Ontario, pausing casually in deep pools, tugging playfully at floating branches, and sliding carefully around protruding rocks. It's a peaceful scene – lush green forest, moss covered rocks, gentle waters.

Although most hikers walk this side trail to see the waterfall, there is other scenery to drink in, and important features in the surrounding woodlands. The trail follows the edge of the 35 acre (14 hectare) Hilton Falls reservoir, enters a silent, cedar grove, and curves through the cedars to a glacial pothole large enough to stand in.

Above Hilton Falls, the trail continues along Sixteen Mile Creek and past a beaver pond before turning inland. As the creek bubbles over its rocky bed, walk quietly along its banks. You may spot an American Water Shrew, an animal only found near cool, clean woodland streams. Mink play around logs jammed up in the creek and raccoons prowl the shallows.

In the woodlands, sugar maples are the dominant trees, but you'll also find white pine regenerating under the hardwoods. Once clearcut, the trees in this area are now staging a comeback in the same forest that once fueled a busy sawmill, now just ruins at the waterfall.

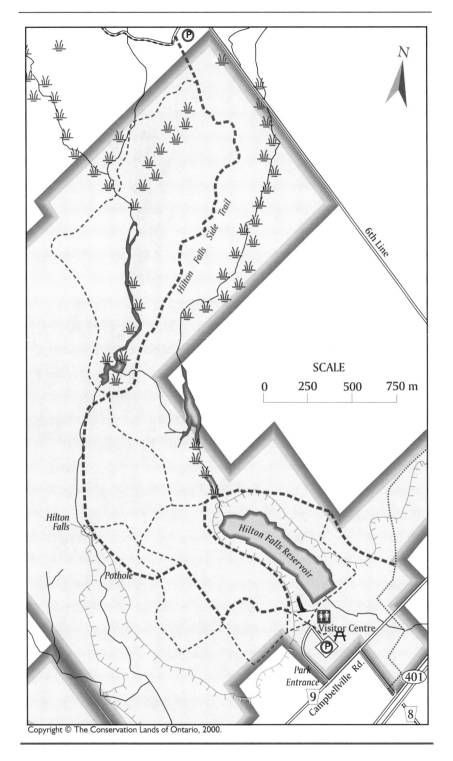

N

SCALE

0   250   500   750 m

6th Line

Hilton Falls Side Trail

Hilton
Falls

Pothole

Hilton Falls Reservoir

Visitor Centre

Park
Entrance

Campbellville Rd.

9

401

8

Copyright © The Conservation Lands of Ontario, 2000.

WALKING FERN
SIDE TRAIL

LOCATION:	Halton Hills
DISTANCE:	1 km (0.6 mile) linear
RATING:	Beginner
BTG:	Toronto, map #13, S. 36.6
HIGHLIGHT:	Large cluster of rare walking ferns

TRAIL SURFACE: Grass, hard packed earth, rocks and a bit of pavement

DIRECTIONS: From the 401, take Hwy. 10 north. Drive through Norval (outside Georgetown) and turn left onto Mayfield Rd. This turns into the Tenth Line. Look for the blue side trail sign on a bend in the road.

Although this trail is short, it's a world unto its own. You can easily linger here for an entire day, walking among lush vegetation, feeling the cool air on a hot summer day, and searching for the rare walking fern.

This path travels through an outlier with a north facing slope. Due to this position, the valley is cool and moist, a habitat unique to this area. It's quiet. Very quiet. A perfect setting for a rare fern.

Nestled among ginger and common polypody, you'll find the walking fern, its leathery fronds casting a trail over limestone boulders. Near a stile towards the end of the trail, you'll find a large cluster of these ferns stepping delicately over one another. Anchored into thick moss, the tiny ferns are so dense that you can hardly see their offshoots.

Make sure you don't walk this whole trail with your head down in search of the fern. The entire valley has a feel onto its own and you're bound to stumble upon a walking fern. The plant is unmistakable once you see it.

Halfway along the valley, the slope starts facing west and the habitat changes completely. It shifts from yellow birch and hemlock in a cool valley, to oak trees growing on a talus slope.

On your return, stop beside one of the rare walking ferns. It's the farthest south you'll ever find one.

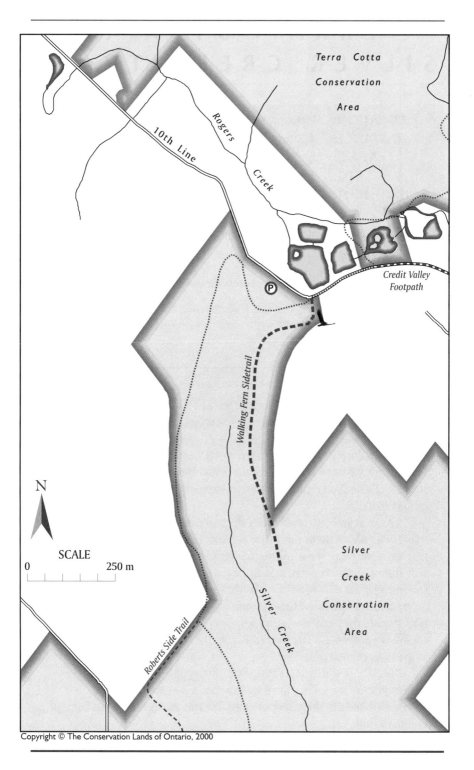

Terra Cotta
Conservation
Area

Rogers

Creek

10th Line

Credit Valley
Footpath

P

Walking Fern Sidetrail

N

SCALE

0   250 m

Silver Creek

Silver
Creek
Conservation
Area

Roberts Side Trail

43

TERRA COTTA TO
SILVER CREEK TRAIL

LOCATION:	Halton Hills
DISTANCE:	4.3 km (2.7 mile) linear
RATING:	Beginner
BTG:	Toronto, map #13, S. 39.5-35.8
HIGHLIGHT:	Environmentally Sensitive Protected Area, wetland, ruins
LINK:	Caledon Trailway

TRAIL SURFACE: Grass, hard packed earth, rocks and a bit of pavement

DIRECTIONS: From the 401, take Hwy. 10 north. Turn left on King St. and drive through Terra Cotta. Turn right on Winston Churchill and follow the signs.

Named after the clay colour, the Terra Cotta region has natural floor tiling. As you descend into the river valley, you eventually walk on Queenstone Shale.

From the Nature Centre at Terra Cotta Conservation Area, take the Alan Coventry Nature Trail to reach the main Bruce trail. As the path heads south, it takes a slow, continuous descent deep into the ancient glacial valley of the Credit River.

As you climb out of the valley the trail reaches an upland portion where two valley systems come together. The cold waters of Roger's Creek flow down the escarpment and meet Silver Creek in the first big field you walk through. At this point, look at the red pathway you're walking on – it's Queenston Shale.

Head toward Silver Creek by crossing the bridge. As you climb the talus slope to the top of the escarpment, you're walking on the bottom of an ancient tropical sea. In fact you can still see the structure where polyps once formed a large coral reef.

Make sure you divert on the Irwin Quarry Side Trail. It leads down stone stairs into the valley. You'll see irregular pieces and flat slabs in the outcrops around the old quarry outcrop. The trail emerges from the forest at Fallbrook Trail.

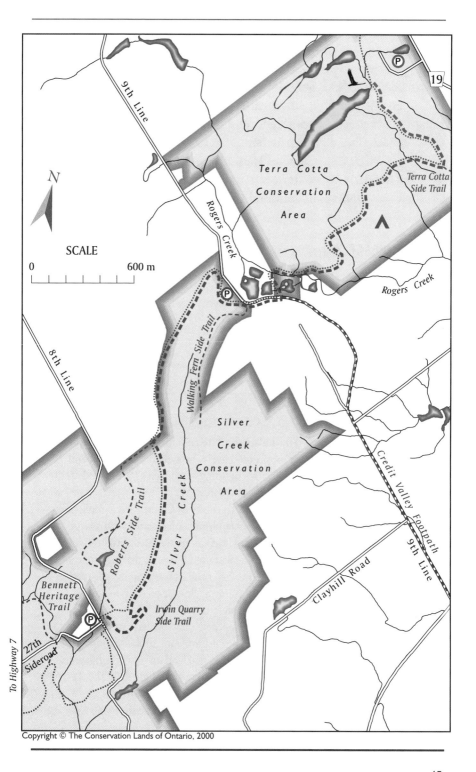

T R I M B L E   T R A I L

LOCATION:	Belfountain Conservation Area, Belfountain
DISTANCE:	3 km linear (1.9 mile) (a 12 km (7.5 mile) loop from Belfountain to Forks of the Credit).
RATING:	Intermediate
BTG:	Caledon Hills, map #13, S. 2.5,
HIGHLIGHT:	Historic site, old heritage road
LINK:	Belfountain Conservation Area trails

TRAIL SURFACE: Gravel, hard packed earth and rocks

DIRECTIONS: From Hwy. 401 take Hwy. 24 north, pass through Erin and turn right on Shaw's Creek Rd. (5th Line West Caledon). Turn left on Bush St. and at the "T" intersection turn left. Follow this road around the corner and down the hill. The Conservation Area is on your right at the bottom of the hill.

MORE INFORMATION: (519) 927-5838. Admission fee applies.

Belfountain was first settled in 1825, when the village was known as Tubtown. A large tub used by a blacksmith to cool forged hot metal stood in the town centre. The area is most noted for its brownstone, quarried and used to construct Ontario's legislative buildings at Queen's Park. A side trail visits the original site of the Crowsnest Quarry.

From the parking lot head towards the West Credit River. You'll pass a grist stone from a former mill, before entering a picnic area with a large fountain. From there, the Trimble Trail leads along the West Credit River. It follows the original Belfountain line, a road used by locals driving horse and buggy to reach the Forks of the Credit. Later the trail leaves this heritage road and continues on one of the old tramway lines used to transport quarried rock to the Credit Valley Railway.

Belfountain Conservation Area was originally owned by Charles W. Mack, a philanthropist who invented the cushion back rubber stamp. This area was his summer retreat and stone stairs still lead up to where his house once stood. On his property, Charles built lookouts and displays: the dam he felt was a miniature Niagara Falls and the caves were a reminder of Yellowstone National Park. A stone pathway leads to these sites.

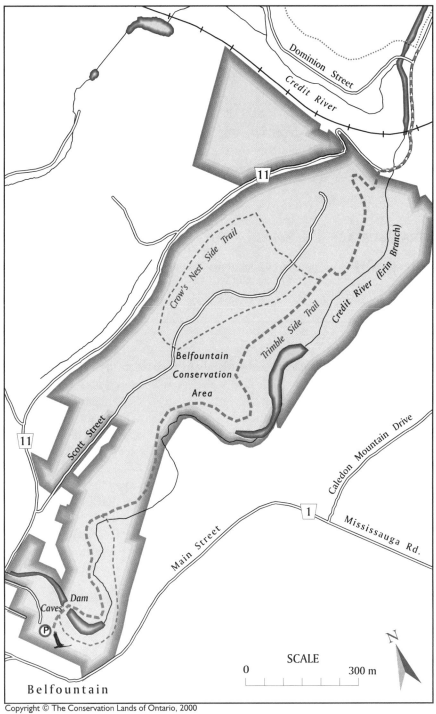

Dominion Street

Credit River

11

Crow's Nest Side Trail

Credit River (Erin Branch)

Belfountain
Conservation
Area

Trimble Side Trail

11

Scott Street

Caledon Mountain Drive

1

Mississauga Rd.

Main Street

Dam

Caves

P

Belfountain

SCALE

0   300 m

N

MEADOW SIDE TRAIL

LOCATION:	Forks of the Credit Provincial Park, Caledon
DISTANCE:	4 km (2.5 mile) loop
RATING:	Beginner
BTG:	Caledon Hills, map #15, meadow to bluff side trail
HIGHLIGHT:	Narrow gorge, oak ridges moraine
LINK:	Elora Cataract Trailway, Grand Valley Trail, Trans Canada Trail

TRAIL SURFACE: Grass, hard packed earth, rocks, and a bit of pavement

DIRECTIONS: From the 401, take Hwy. 24 north. Turn right on McLaren Road and follow signs for the Provincial Park.

The rolling landscape and kettle lake in this park are the massive deposits and depressions left behind as glaciers scoured this region. It's the end of the oak ridges moraine.

Cutting through the park is the East Credit River, dropping approximately 68 metres (223 feet) from the north to south end of the park, meeting up with the West Credit at the "fork." At this point it becomes the Credit River.

From the parking lot, follow the meadow side trail past the kettle lake, and through wide open meadows that feel like the prairies. You'll also pass farm ruins and abandoned apple orchard trees.

To reach the falls, turn right onto the main trail and then follow the Bluff Side Trail. At the falls, the rocks represent the boundary of two geological time periods: the grey sandstone of the whirlpool formation and the red shale of the Queenston Formation.

If you want to reach the "fork," continue on the main Bruce Trail at the Bluff Trail intersection and walk through the river gorge until you reach the Forks of the Credit Road. This trail portion follows an old road allowance. You can take the Brimstone Side Trail back to the parking lot.

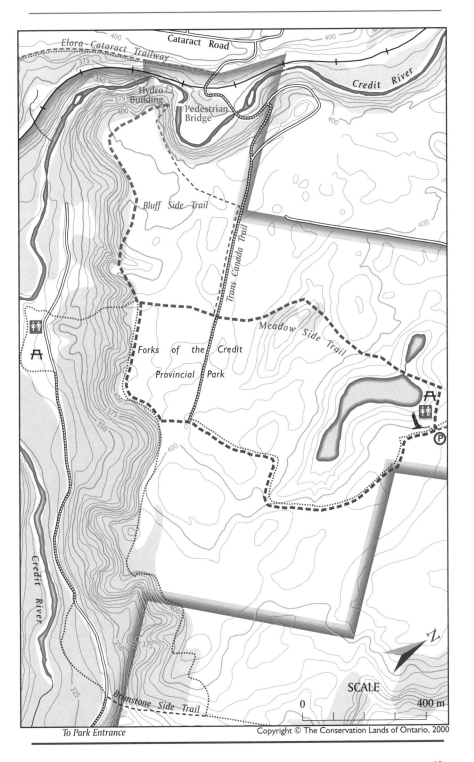

ALBION HILLS TRAIL

LOCATION:	Albion Hills Conservation Area, Palgrave
DISTANCE:	2.1 km (1.3 mile) linear
RATING:	Beginner
BTG:	Caledon, map #17, S. 40.8-38.7
HIGHLIGHT:	Oak Ridges Moraine
LINK:	Caledon Trailway, Humber Valley Heritage Trail

TRAIL SURFACE: Grass, hard packed earth, rocks and a bit of pavement

DIRECTIONS: From Hwy. 401, take Hwy. 27 north to Highway 50. The Conservation Area entrance is on Hwy. 50, 8 km north of Bolton.

MORE INFORMATION: (905) 854-0234. Admission fee applies.

The Oak Ridges Moraine is an important bioregion for the communities and rural areas that live along its border. Aside from providing a rolling hill landscape with forests, fields, wetlands and lakes, the moraine supplies drinking water and is the source of thirty rivers and streams.

Albion Hills plays an important role in the Humber River Valley, a water system that links Lake Ontario to the Oak Ridges Moraine and the Niagara Escarpment. Visit the Conservation Area's 516 hectares (1,275 acres) in late fall, when meadows bloom with asters and goldenrod, and views across the rolling Caledon Hills are most colourful.

From the nature centre, walk down the hill toward Taylor's Pond. From the docks, a Conservation Area trail leads through a pine plantation and follows the south edge of the pond. You're bound to see a variety of migratory waterfowl here during the fall.

The trail continues to an old railway bed and follows the Caledon Trailway. Near Patterson Side Road, the Bruce Trail leaves the Trailway bed. Descend the stairs at the railway bridge and look for the blazes on the trees.

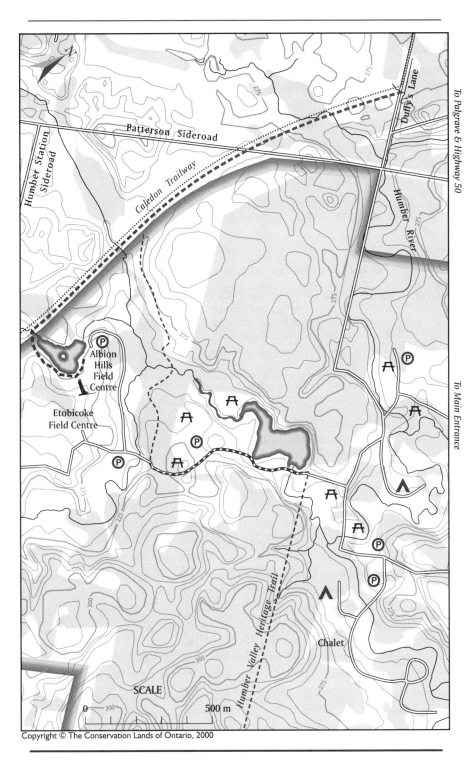

SCALE

0   500 m

Copyright © The Conservation Lands of Ontario, 2000

PALGRAVE TRAIL

LOCATION:	Palgrave Conservation Area, Palgrave
DISTANCE:	4 km loop (2.5 mile) (Other area trails: 16 kilometres (10 miles) of ski trails, from a 3.6 km (2.2 mile) beginner's loop to a 8.4 km (5.2 mile) advanced loop)
RATING:	Beginner
BTG:	Caledon Hills, map #17, S. 42.8
HIGHLIGHT:	Oak Ridges Moraine

TRAIL SURFACE: Grass, hard packed earth, rocks and a bit of pavement

DIRECTIONS: From Hwy. 401, take Hwy. 27 north to Highway 50. Approximately one kilometre (0.62 mile) north of Palgrave, after a curve in the road, you'll see the entrance on your left. It's not well marked so slow down.

As the last glacier moved over Ontario, scouring the landscape with its icy tongue, it gathered the material it removed – sand, gravel and other debris. These piles of rubble were either deposited by meltwater or stacked into mounds that remained after the ice melted.

This is the Oak Ridges Moraine, a 200 kilometre (124 mile) narrow ridge of glacial debris that formed the rolling Caledon landscape as much as the surrounding sandy plains, kettle lakes and wetlands. You'll get a sense of this varying terrain in Palgrave Conservation Area. The trail winds its way over hills and through valleys, among woodlands dominated with eastern white cedar, sugar maple and white ash. If you take some of the side trails you'll also see a kettle lake, meadows and wetland areas.

Follow the laneway that leads away from the highway. Before you enter a former parking lot which is now a large open area, take the first trail to your left. This will connect with the Bruce Trail.

Best known for its ski trails, winter is a good time to try this trail. There are 16 kilometres (10 miles) of groomed trails that wind throughout the forest and link through loops to the Bruce Trail.

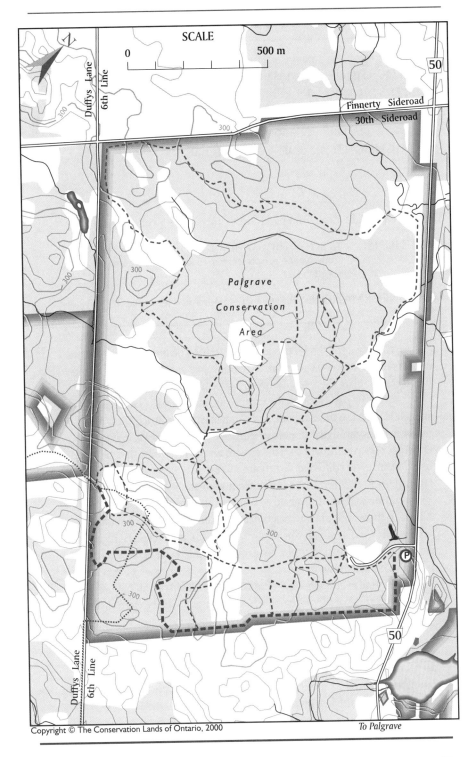

To Palgrave

G L E N   H A F F Y   T R A I L

LOCATION:	Glen Haffy Conservation Area, Mono Mills
DISTANCE:	3.2 km (2 mile) linear
RATING:	Beginner
BTG:	Caledon, map #18, S. 53.8-52.2
HIGHLIGHT:	Scenic views, fish hatchery

TRAIL SURFACE: Grass, hard packed earth, rocks and a bit of pavement

DIRECTIONS: From Hwy. 401, take Hwy. 427 to Hwy. 7/Airport Rd. The Conservation Area is located 10 km (6 miles) north of Caledon East.

MORE INFORMATION: (905) 854-0234. Admission fee applies.

The Prayer of the Woods starts this trail. The inspirational phrase appears in forest preserves in Portugal, but is just as valid here. Stop to read it and contemplate these words as you walk through this woodland trail.

From the parking lot, take the Conservation Area's Nature Trail where stairs lead down to the campsite and connect with the Bruce Trail. The pathway leads through a woodland threaded by streams. Various bridge crossings take you from one scenic view to another: streams that run over boulders from two different directions and meet underneath the bridge to a magical hemlock forest that ascends from a stream.

Unmarked side trails lead to scenic spots of the rolling Caledon Hills. Although there aren't many rock outcrops visible and the surrounding area is rolling hills and farmland, you are on escarpment land. Glen Haffy is located along the central portion of the Niagara Escarpment where few exposures of bedrock strata are visible.

The trail eventually exits onto Glen Haffy Road. From here you can retrace your steps or follow the blue blazes along the road to join the main trail in a 10.5 km (6.5 mile) loop.

One mile down from the Bruce Trail is a spring of cold water that percolates from the hillside. It's the location of a fish hatchery where trout are reared in the barn's holding tanks. Fishing is allowed in the fishing ponds located in the Conservation Area, not to be confused with the holding tanks situated at the hatchery.

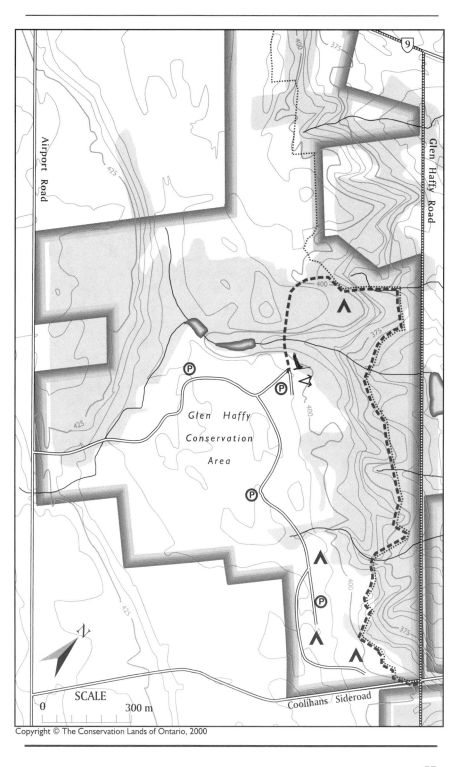

Airport Road

Glen Haffy Road

9

425

400

375

400

375

Glen Haffy

Conservation

Area

425

400

400

375

SCALE

0   300 m

Coolihans Sideroad

Copyright © The Conservation Lands of Ontario, 2000

CLIFFTOP SIDE TRAIL

LOCATION: Mono Cliffs Provincial Park, Mono Centre
DISTANCE: 3 km (1.9 mile) loop
RATING: Intermediate
BTG: Dufferin, map #19,
HIGHLIGHT: Outliers, viewing platform, crevice descent

TRAIL SURFACE: Gravel, hard packed earth and rocks

DIRECTIONS: From Hwy. 401 take Hwy. 10 north towards Orangeville, turn East (right) at Camilla onto County Rd. 8. Drive through the hamlet of Mono Centre and the Park will be on your left. You must use the parking lot on 3rd Line.

MORE INFORMATION: (705) 435-4331. Admission fee applies.

In Mono Cliffs Provincial Park, the Niagara Escarpment runs along the 4.5 kilometre (three mile) length of the park and rises to a height of over 500 metres (1640 feet) above sea level. Throughout its trail system, you walk through a glacial spillway separating two isolated rock outliers from the main escarpment, pass deep crevice caves, and walk on top of 40 metre (131 foot) cliffs.

Part of the trail system is formed by old roads and carriage trails. Along with stonewalls, scattered orchard trees and farmstead ruins, there are remains of a local Irish settlement that grew to 2,200 by 1850.

The hike begins on the park's Carriage Trail, then connects with the main Bruce Trail and heads north. When you reach the blue blazes, continue on the Clifftop Side Trail. At each intersection, stay to your left to continue on this trail. A viewing platform further along the trail offers a grand view of the outliers, cliff face, and spillway stretching below. The highlight is Jacob's Ladder, a wooden staircase with interpretive signs that descends into a crevice. By connecting with a park trail, this is also a shortcut back to the parking lot.

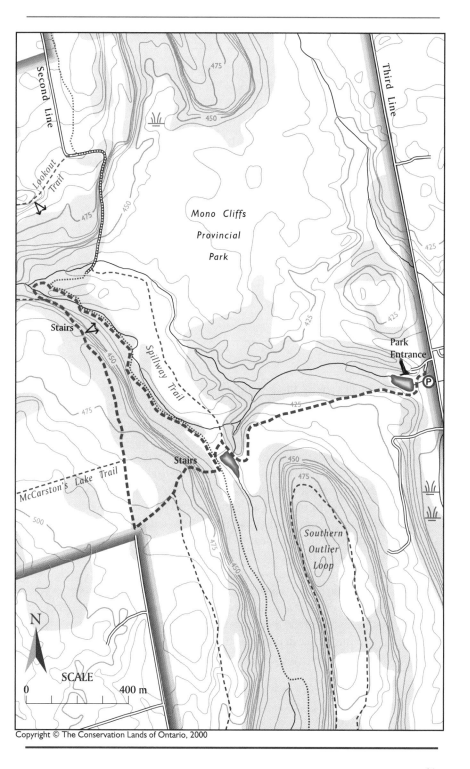

Second Line

Third Line

475

450

Mono Cliffs

Provincial

Park

475

450

425

425

425

Lookout Trail

Stairs

Spillway Trail

Park
Entrance

P

450

475

575

425

McCarston's Lake Trail

Stairs

450

475

500

450

575

475

Southern
Outlier
Loop

475

450

N

SCALE

0   400 m

PRIMROSE LOOP

LOCATION: Primrose Loop, Primrose (Boyne Valley Provincial Park)

DISTANCE: 5.5 km (3.4 mile) loop

BTG: Dufferin, map # 20, loop trail to section 15.3

HIGHLIGHT: One of the best panoramic views. The pinnacle (high point along a lateral moraine)

TRAIL SURFACE: Hard packed earth, rocks, grass

DIRECTIONS: From Hwy. 401, take Hwy. 24 toward Primrose. At Hwy. 89, continue straight through on Mulmur Township Line 1 WHS. The parking lot is 1.1 km (0.7 mile) on your right hand side.

If you like apples, this is your trail. You'll walk through more old apple orchards than on any other section of the Bruce Trail. On every few steps you can pick another apple to eat. If you like high, panoramic lookout points, this is also your trail.

The short loop through Boyne Valley Provincial Park is closed in by evergreens and descends through a large milkweed field, great for spotting monarch butterflies in the fall. The trail then leads to Pinnacle Hill, with a panoramic view of the region. Dark green wooded sections outline the farm fields and pastures, and on a clear day, the blue of Nottawasaga Bay spreads into the distance. From here you head through a forest into the largest old apple orchard on the trail.

On this trail you'll also walk past a dying pine plantation. If you sit still here long enough, you can watch the light move through the forest. You'll see it drip off the branches, then dust the trees as a light snowfall does. The forest seems fragile and delicate as it turns from a soft pink in the morning to dusky purple in the early afternoon.

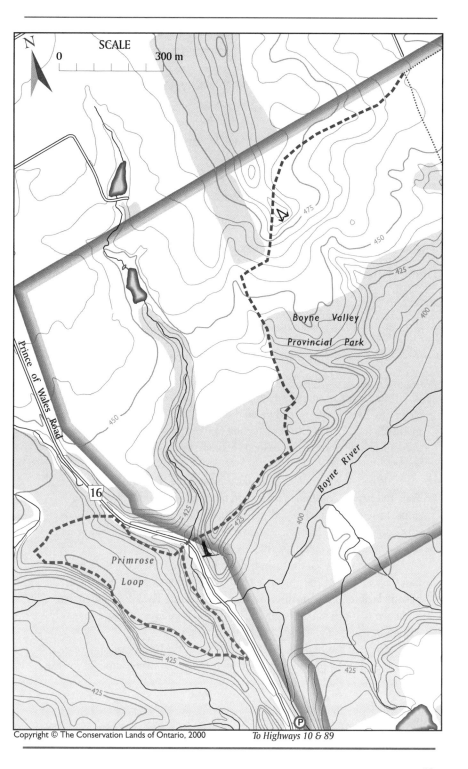

SCALE

0   300 m

Prince of Wales Road

16

475

450

425

400

Boyne Valley
Provincial Park

Boyne River

450

425

Primrose
Loop

425

425

425

425

K E Y H O L E   T R A I L

LOCATION:	Keyhole Trail (Nottawasaga Bluffs Conservation Area, Singhampton)
DISTANCE:	4.3 km (2.8 mile) loop
BTG:	Blue Mountain, map #22, Nottawasaga Access Trail to 19.9
HIGHLIGHT:	Deep crevices and canyon like walls to walk through, freedom rock

TRAIL SURFACE: Gravel, hard packed earth and rocks

DIRECTIONS: From the 401, take County Rd. 124 (formerly Hwy. 24) toward Singhampton. Turn south onto Milltown Rd. and an immediate left onto Ewing Rd. Turn left onto Sideroad 17/18 and turn left onto Nottawasaga Concession #10. The parking lot is 500 metres (1640 feet) on your right.

Caves and crevices have long been a mystery to human beings. The chance to discover one is the lure on this trail. You walk at the base of six metre (20 foot) outliers that create mini canyons. Formed by meltwater, these rocks split and curve into long channels, leading you deep into another world.

Where the Keyhole Side Trail turns from the Nottawasaga Access Trail, the canyon continues farther and farther. The pathway leads up a slope through large rock boulders, passes through small crevices and ends with a tight squeeze through a small hole in the wall. There is a way around this keyhole if you can't quite fit.

When you reach the main trail, continue on to Freedom Rock and Best Caves. Some of the phrases etched into Freedom Rock are weathered, but still legible: "Individualists are Diamonds", and "The Education System is bloated to much junk thought." These strong statements were apparently written by a hermit who used to live in the area.

On your return, look for the blue blaze of the Nottawasaga Access Trail. It leads back to the parking lot, or, if the lure is strong enough, you can return to the Keyhole.

SCALE

0   500 m

15 - 16 Sideroad

McKinney's Hill

Keyhole Side Trail

Best Caves

Freedom Rock

N

DEVIL'S GLEN
PROVINCIAL PARK TRAIL

LOCATION:	Devil's Glen Provincial Park, Singhampton
DISTANCE:	1.9 km (1.2 mile) linear
BTG:	Blue Mountain, map #22, S. 25.2-23.3
HIGHLIGHT:	Best fall vistas
LINK:	Ganaraska Trail

TRAIL SURFACE: Hard packed earth, rocks

DIRECTIONS: From Hwy. 401, take Hwy. 24 north toward Collingwood. Look for provincial park signs on your right a few kilometres or miles outside of Singhampton.

One of the highest peaks along the escarpment is 460 metres (1509 feet) above sea level. Before starting on this trail, walk to the lookout platform at Devil's Glen Provincial Park and admire the steep bedrock gorge at the edge of the escarpment. The highest location in Southern Ontario, reaching an elevation of approximately 546 metres (1791 feet) above sea level, lies about four kilometres (2.5 miles) to the northwest on the Singhampton moraine, looking at Edward Lake.

The view from the platform sweeps over the entire valley, and is especially scenic when fall colours spread across the lower walls. Devil's Glen rests on a broad terrace known as the Manitoulin Bedrock Ledge, the site of a glacial meltwater channel that flowed along the edge of the escarpment.

The gorge, carved by the Mad River spreads as far as your eye can see. The upper rim along the gorge is lined by Silurian Amabel dolomite caprock, a form of limestone. The lower valley walls are steep and covered with dense deciduous forest, and formed bedrock fragments called talus. Although you may not see them, the provincially rare harts tongue and smooth cliff brake ferns are found on these steep cliffs.

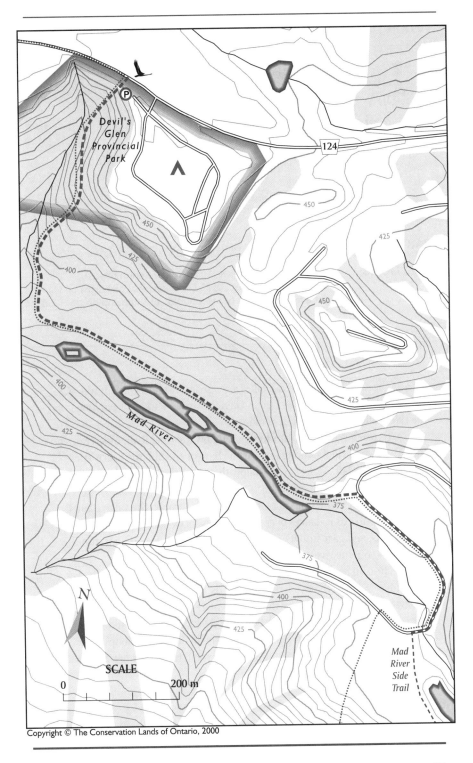

Devil's
Glen
Provincial
Park

124

Mad River

400

N

SCALE

0   200 m

Mad
River
Side
Trail

MAD RIVER SIDE TRAIL

LOCATION:	Devil's Glen Provincial Park, Singhampton
DISTANCE:	5.8 km (3.6 mile) loop
RATING:	Intermediate
BTG:	Blue Mountain, map #22
HIGHLIGHT:	Outlooks, steep descent into the Mad River Valley
LINK:	Ganaraska Trail

TRAIL SURFACE: Gravel, hard packed earth and rocks

DIRECTIONS: From Hwy. 401, take Hwy. 10 to Hwy. 24 north toward Collingwood. Look for Devil's Glen provincial park signs on your right a few kilometres or miles outside of Singhampton.

The Mad River Side Trail takes a steep descent into Glen Huron. From the lookout platform at Devil's Glen Provincial Park, you can look into the river valley where you'll be walking.

To reach the base of this lookout, follow the Mad River Side Trail sign from the Devil's Glen parking lot. At the base of the hill, the Bruce Trail veers off to the left. Make sure to follow that, even though another trail sign is marked as the Mad River Trail.

This trail follows the Mad River as it cuts through the valley. You'll follow its course as it dances over rapids, cross its wetland areas on boardwalks, and gaze into its rocky bottom from a bridge. It's a tranquil pathway – you, the river, and a dense forest.

The trail leads to a parking lot at the base of the ski hill. Walk over the bridge and pass the two irrigation ponds. You'll see a sign for the four kilometre Glen Huron Trail or the 6.5 kilometre Escarpment loop. Follow the blazes that lead to a straight trail along the river. This wide section eventually leads to the Glen Huron Pond. The pathway then loops back on county roads. At the top of 15/16 sideroad, you'll have a panoramic lookout over Glen Huron.

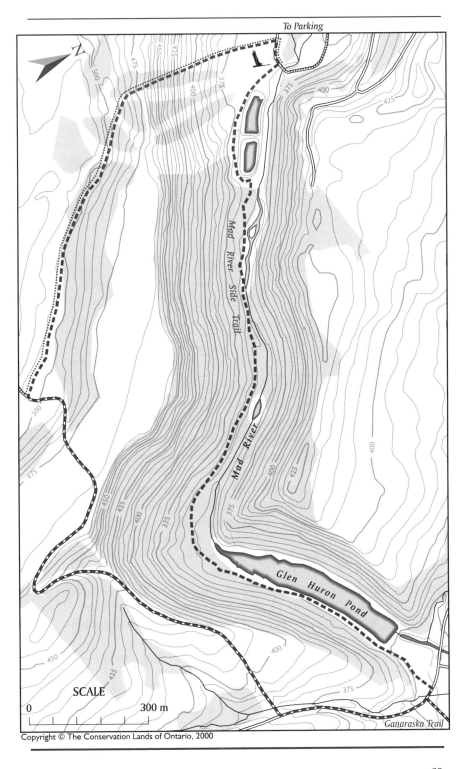

To Parking

N

Mad River Side Trail

Mad River

Glen Huron Pond

SCALE

0   300 m

Ganaraska Trail

Copyright © The Conservation Lands of Ontario, 2000

69

PETUN CONSERVATION AREA TRAIL

LOCATION:	Petun Conservation Area, Osler Bluff
DISTANCE:	3.9 km (2.4 mile) loop
BTG:	Blue Mountain, map #23, S. 48.1-52
HIGHLIGHT:	Highest section on the Bruce Trail, former native grounds

TRAIL SURFACE: Gravel, hard packed earth and rocks

DIRECTIONS: From the 401, drive Hwy. 24 toward Collingwood. After Nottawasaga, turn left on Nottawasaga 36/37 Sideroad. It becomes Collingwood/Clearview Townline. Turn left on Grey Rd. 19 and then turn left on 2nd line. Parking is 100 metres (328 ft) up from the Petun Conservation Area entrance (12 km or 0.9 mi from Grey Rd. 19).

For years, the Petun nation lived in this area, with their longhouses and tobacco fields where open meadows now lie, their hunting grounds within the forest, their fishing and water source in the Black Ash Creek.

Think about them as you look at the Black Ash Creek valley below this trail. This Conservation Area was named in their honour. An Iroquois speaking people noted for cultivating tobacco, the Petun were a smaller nation that lived along the slopes of the Niagara Escarpment. The influx of Europeans decimated this nation with an outbreak of smallpox in the 1600s. Thereafter they were dispersed by a war with the Seneca Nation and eventually settled in Oklahoma in the 1850s. They are now known as the "Wyandot."

Walk the Petun trail in early summer or fall (the children's summer camps start in July and August). It's a quiet trail and as you peer into the Black Ash Creek valley, you can imagine the world of the Petun. You'll also see the world of European settlers among the huge field stones cleared from fields. Along the corn fields you'll see clusters of milkweed, a great spot to see monarch butterflies. Four kilometres south of Petun, the Bruce Trail reaches its highest point at 540 metres (1480 feet).

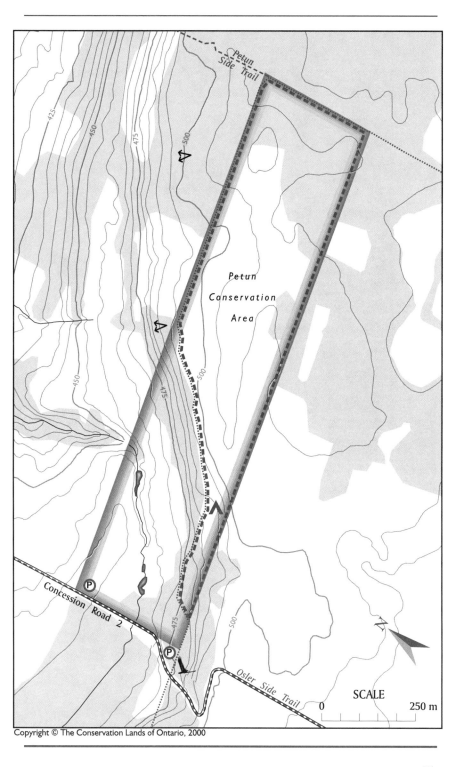

Petun
Side Trail

Petun
Conservation
Area

Concession Road 2

Osler Side Trail

SCALE

0   250 m

KOLAPORE
UPLANDS TRAIL

LOCATION:	Kolapore Uplands, Collingwood
DISTANCE:	9 km (5.6 mile) loop
RATING:	Advanced
BTG:	Beaver Valley, map #25, S. 27.2 - 33.7
HIGHLIGHT:	30 metre high (98 foot) gorge to walk through, pinnacle rock, Duncan Crevice Caves Provincial Nature Reserve

DIRECTIONS: From Hwy. 401, take Hwy. 10/24 north toward Collingwood. Before Singhampton, turn left on Grey Rd. 4 and right on Grey Rd. 2. Turn right on Grey Rd. 19. It becomes 9th Side Road. Continue along 9th Side Road until you see the parking lot for Duncan Crevice Caves (2.2 km or 1.4 mi from the 10th Line junction).

Although the underground world is perceived as durable, caves are sensitive areas. This trail starts at Duncan Crevice Caves, where distinctive fern, moss, liverwort, and lichen vegetation is one of the best developed and preserved on the Niagara escarpment.

Walking off the trail can displace moss cushions, trample the humus layer and otherwise disturb this fragile vegetation. Please stay only on the trail and tighten the rein on your dog's leash in this area. Resist the temptation to walk into long channels you can see through. You'll have a chance later as this trail leads through a 30 metre (98 foot) gorge to the summit of Metcalfe Rock. The excitement continues with creek and scree crossings.

The lookouts over Metcalfe Rock offer a panoramic view of the Kolapore Creek Valley. After you pass a waterfall and meadow, make sure you follow the blaze to your right (there's another road leading straight ahead, which takes you to Metcalfe Rock but doesn't complete the loop). Soon thereafter you walk and rock scramble through Metcalfe Rock, filled with little caves, rock outcroppings and long tree roots straddling rocks.

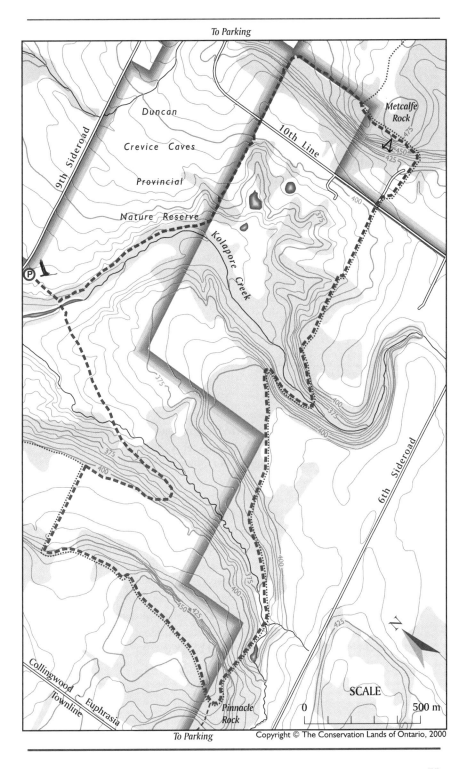

Duncan

Crevice Caves

Provincial

Nature Reserve

9th Sideroad

10th Line

Metcalfe Rock

Kolapore Creek

6th Sideroad

400

375

375

400

400

375

375

450 425

400

425

Collingwood Euphrasia Townline

Pinnacle Rock

SCALE

0   500 m

N

Copyright © The Conservation Lands of Ontario, 2000

WALTER'S FALLS TRAIL

LOCATION:	Walter's Falls
DISTANCE:	4.1 km (2.5 mile) linear
RATING:	Beginner
BTG:	Sydenham, map #29, S. 7.7-11.8
HIGHLIGHT:	Pastoral, creek crossing, Southern Ontario farmland scene

TRAIL SURFACE: Hard packed earth, grass

DIRECTIONS: From the 401 West, take Hwy. 10 north towards Owen Sound. After Markdale, turn right onto Holland Euphrasia Townline towards Walter's Falls. At the junction of Grey Rd. 40 and 29, continue on Grey Rd. 29 to Bognor. Drive through Walter's Falls. Turn left on the 2nd Sydenham Township Concession (at the stop sign) and drive to the top of the hill (1.3 km from the stop sign).

This trail crosses typical southern Ontario landscape, cow pastures, old apple trees, and crop fields. In fact, whatever season you visit, summer or fall, there is a treat waiting. From wildberry bushes to apple trees, you can spot the fruits from far off.

A panoramic view of the area on a high point of land is your first point of reference. Then you dip into the forest to cross creeks and walk beside a babbling brook, stroll through a sea of jewelweed, and pass an old stone farm foundation with former apple orchard trees. You'll walk through a cow pasture where one or two cows are sure to pick up their heads and stare at you, chew a bit and then look down again.

Eventually you'll walk through typical escarpment property with limestone cliffs, moss covered boulders and dense fern clusters. If you want to take a longer hike, continue to Anthea's Waterfall, a cascading waterfall that seems to hug the rocks it passes around before entering the creek below.

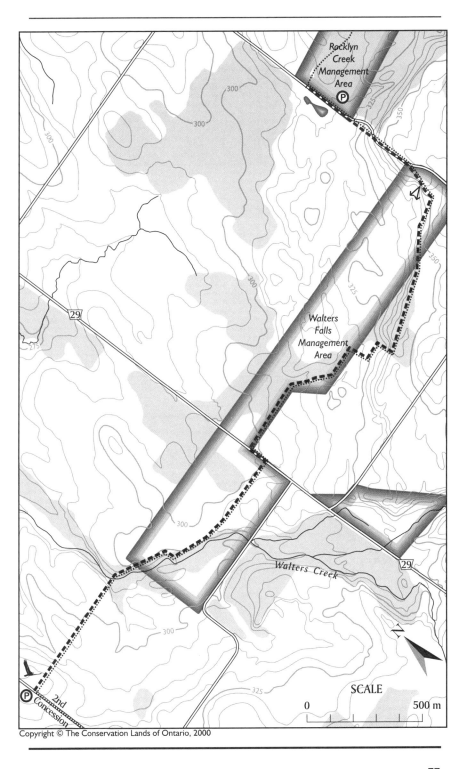

Rocklyn
Creek
Management
Area
Ⓟ

Walters
Falls
Management
Area

29

29

Walters Creek

SCALE

0   500 m

Ⓟ 2nd
Concession

77

THE GLEN TRAIL

LOCATION:	The Glen Management Area, Benallen
DISTANCE:	3.3-km (2 mile) linear
RATING:	Beginner
BTG:	Sydenham, map #31, S. 61.0-57.7
HIGHLIGHT:	Glen

TRAIL SURFACE: Hard packed earth, grass and rocks

DIRECTIONS: From the 401 West, take Hwy. 6 North towards Owen Sound. Turn north on Hwy. 6 through Springmount. Turn right on Derby Sarawak line and left on Gordon Sutherland Parkway. At the stop sign in Benallen the Parkway turns into Grey Rd. 17. The parking lot is located 3.8 km (2.4 mile) from this point.

SPECIAL CONSIDERATIONS:
Seasonal hunting. Call Grey Sauble Conservation Authority (519) 376-3076.

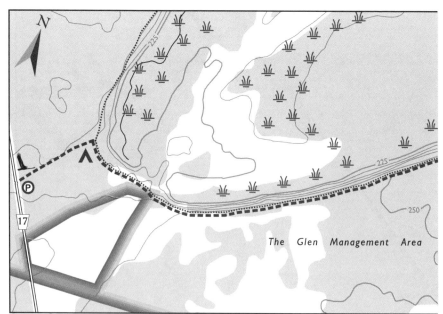

The Glen Management Area

Copyright © The Conservation Lands of Ontario, 2000

The Glen rises 15 to 20 metres (49 to 66 feet) above what used to be the former bays of Lake Algonquin. Now it rises above a sea of trees. From the lookout point, if you watch the trees swaying in the wind, you can imagine the waves of a warm, tropical sea.

Parallel to this limestone ridge extends a deep trough, carved by wave action of glacial waters. This trail follows this cliff edge, looking down on treetops, and ancient barrier beach ridges along the base of the escarpment. It also crosses over deep crevices and exposed stretches of bedrock scratched by the glacier as it gouged the area. These crevice step-overs aren't wide and the narrow chasms offer a chance to cross even for those afraid of heights. In fact, the rocks are kind throughout this trail. In the few areas where there's an uphill climb, the rocks form natural steps.

To reach the Glen, follow the side trail and turn right. You'll walk through thick woods most of the way before reaching an open field area. When you reach the cedar and maple forest, it's time to turn around. On your return, after you've reached the campsite area, make sure you follow the blue trail to return to your car.

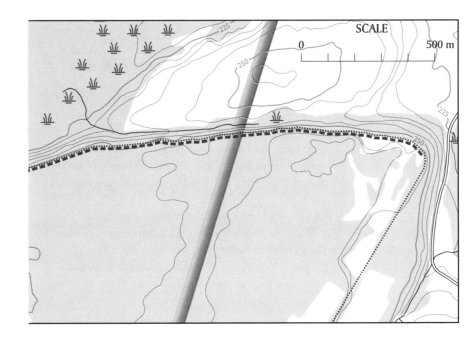

KEMBLE MOUNTAIN
SIDE TRAIL

LOCATION:	Kemble Mountain Management Area, Kemble
DISTANCE:	7.1 km (4.4 mile) loop
RATING:	Beginner
BTG:	Sydenham, map #32
HIGHLIGHT:	A high concentration of rare ferns

TRAIL SURFACE: Hard packed earth with rocks and grass

DIRECTIONS: From 401 West, take Hwy. 6 north toward Owen Sound. In the city turn left at 10th St. E., drive through town and over a bridge to turn right at Second Ave. W. This road eventually turns into Grey Rd. One. You'll come to a stop sign in the village of Kemble. Drive straight through and continue on to Concession 20 (don't follow Grey Rd. One towards Wiarton). The hill you see from the intersection is Kemble Mountain. When you drive up the crest of the hill, you'll see Bruce Trail blazes on your left. Park on the side of the road.

Kemble Mountain clutches two rare fern species, seldom found in such abundance on one trail. With the fallen leaves contrasting in colour, autumn is one of the best times to discover these ferns.

It's in the dimly lit rock crevices that you'll see the Hart's Tongue (Phyllitis Scolopendrium), a rare fern that grows in rubble and loose rocks that have fallen away from the escarpment. Often found with its leathery leaves splayed against the walls of a crevice, this evergreen has a distinct shape that can't be confused with another fern. So does the Northern Holly Fern (Polystichum Lonchitis), the other rare fern found in abundance on this trail.

The start of this footpath is a bit rough and requires balancing around and over large limestone boulders. The path is smoother once you pass a plaque erected in memory of Robert Samuel Edmonston, the individual who sold the property to the Grey Sauble Conservation Authority. As the footpath nears the road, you can cross the road to a trail on the other side and follow the escarpment edge to a lookout point.

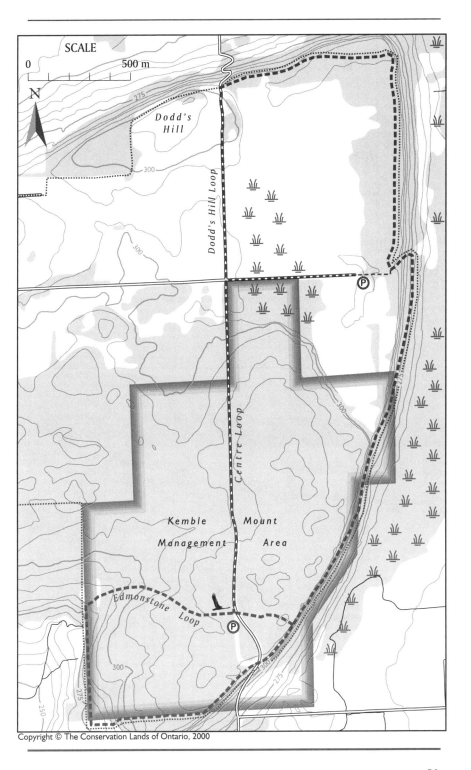

81

SKINNER'S BLUFF TRAIL

LOCATION:	Bruce's Caves Conservation Area, Oxenden
DISTANCE:	7.4 km (4.6 mile) linear
RATING:	Beginner
BTG:	Peninsula, map #34, S. 24.5-31.0
HIGHLIGHT:	Scenic lookouts, ancient sea caves

TRAIL SURFACE: Hard packed earth, grass and rocks

DIRECTIONS: From the 401 West, take Hwy. 6 North through Owen Sound to Wiarton. In Wiarton, turn right onto Frank St. (Grey County Rd. 26) and right on Bruce's Caves Rd. Keep to the left through Oxenden.

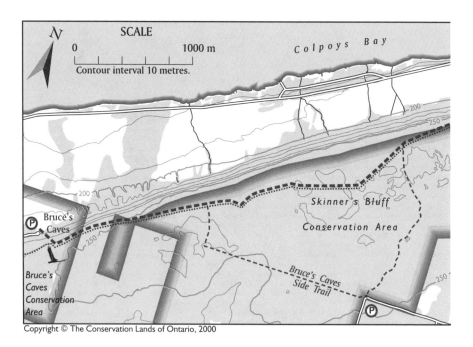

82

If you follow the bend into the forest, eventually you'll walk along Skinner's Bluff, a long escarpment face that casts its view over White Cloud, Griffiths and Hay Island. These lonely islands seem to magically appear, each raising its head above the blue waters towards the end of the trail. It's the pot of gold at the end of an old logging road.

For the first few kilometres, the waters tease you. While walking the old logging road, you can see the distant blue peeking through the trees. It takes a long time to reach the lookout points, but it's well worth the walk.

You'll look down on houses, fields and forest, walk by open meadows, and pause by cedar rail fences lined with old orchard apple trees. And you'll step away from the escarpment edge, so far at one lookout point, that you almost see 360 degrees around you.

On your return, don't forget to walk the trail to Bruce's Caves. One of the few ancient sea caverns that remains completely natural on a trail, there are no stairs or viewing platforms. You can rock scramble your way to every corner of this cavern.

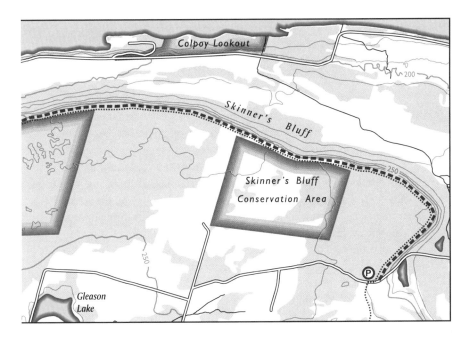

JONES BLUFF
SIDE TRAIL

LOCATION: Cape Croker
DISTANCE: 7.4 km (4.6 mile) loop
RATING: Beginner
BTG: Peninsula, map #34, S. 24.5-31.0
HIGHLIGHT: Scenic lookouts and bird's eye view of
Sydney Bluff

TRAIL SURFACE: Hard packed earth, rocks, grass

DIRECTIONS: From Hwy. 401, take Hwy. 6 North through Owen Sound towards
Tobermory. Turn right on Bruce Cty. Rd. 9, right on Bruce Cty. Rd.
18 and left on Purple Valley Rd. Turn right on McIver Rd. and right
on Boundary Rd. (first road on your right or 1.5 km (.9 mile) from
MacIver Rd.

If you want to feel the way a bird does, take this trail. Look over
MacGregor Harbour where Cape Croker juts into the waters. Then, turn
your head to see Sydney Bluff and Cape Dundas, and Barrier Island in the
distance. The shoreline from Sydney Bay to MacGregor Harbour spreads in
front of you.

On many Bruce Trail walks, hikers hope the rush of the breeze
through the trees means they're near the water. On this trail, although it
never reaches the shoreline, you hear the waves lapping the beaches . . . they
seem to rise up towards you.

Some of the outcrops are large rocky areas where you can walk to a
few different lookout points in one large open section. On others, you
actually see the space in between a rock you're standing on, and the actual
escarpment edge. Even while in the forest you see the bluffs through the
trees and the wide expanse of the open water directly in front of you.

As you round the loop, you'll see the beginning part of Colpoys Bay
and the next entrance harbour of the neighbouring bay. You also see Hay
Island slowly inch forward as you move around the bluff, and then White
Cloud and Griffiths Island in the distance, as you walk above Colpoys Bay.

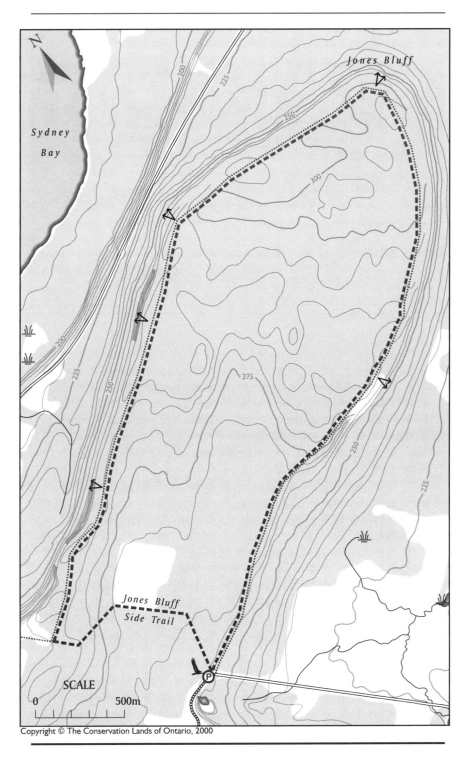

Sydney
Bay

Jones Bluff

Jones Bluff
Side Trail

SCALE

0   500m

Copyright © The Conservation Lands of Ontario, 2000

G U N   P O I N T   L O O P

LOCATION:	Lion's Head
DISTANCE:	4.7 km (2.9 mile) linear
RATING:	Intermediate
BTG:	Peninsula, map #36, S. 68.4-63.7
HIGHLIGHT:	Most lookout points along a short section

TRAIL SURFACE: Hard packed earth, rocks, grass

DIRECTIONS: From Hwy. 401, take Hwy. 6 North through Owen Sound towards Tobermory. Turn right on Bruce Cty. Rd. 9 and follow it to Lion's Head. Turn right on Cemetery Rd. and look for the blue blaze.

There are almost as many overlooks as you take steps on this trail. You'll walk to the cliff edge more on this section than any other trail in this book. You'll reach areas where the rock spreads out far with little vegetation. It offers a wide, open view. Other times you reach triple overlooks – each time you turn around a tree cluster, there is another large outcrop to step onto.

Gun Point isn't the outcrop with the largest, widest lookout. It isn't even one of the ones you might walk to, but it's the one where you see Lion's Head and White Bluff at one end, look across Barrow Bay to Cape Dundas on the other, and even see Barrier Island and Cape Croker in the distance.

It's strange to think when you're sitting on top of these lookout points that they were once underwater, carved and molded into a point by ancient glacial seas. There is much time for such thought on this trail, as you descend and ascend, and briefly turn inland between lookout points. This is a great trail to walk on a hot summer day because much of forest trail is covered and cool, and you receive a strong breeze from the bay at the many lookout points.

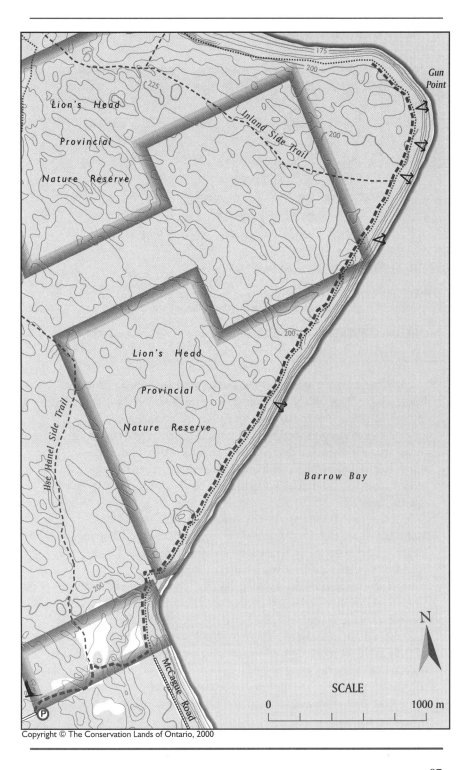

Gun Point

Lion's Head

Provincial

Nature Reserve

Inland Side Trail

Lion's Head

Provincial

Nature Reserve

Use Hanel Side Trail

Barrow Bay

McCague Road

175
200
225
200
200
200

N

SCALE

0   1000 m

P

Copyright © The Conservation Lands of Ontario, 2000

C A V E   P O I N T   T R A I L

LOCATION:	Bruce Peninsula National Park, Tobermory
DISTANCE:	4.8 km (3 mile) linear (Other area trails: 1 km (0.62 mile) Horse Lake, 5 km (3.1 mile) Cyprus Trail)
RATING:	Advanced
BTG:	Peninsula, map #39, S. 132.7 - 137.5
HIGHLIGHT:	Several rock beaches, most challenging section on the Bruce Trail
LINK:	Bruce Peninsula National Park trails

TRAIL SURFACE: Hard packed earth, rocks, grass

DIRECTIONS: To park at Halfway Log Dump, from Hwy. 6, turn right on Emmett Lake Rd. and left on Halfway Log Dump Rd.

MORE INFORMATION: Bruce Peninsula National Park (519) 596-2233.

When you start at Halfway Log Dump, make sure you walk to the beach, a bay of blue set against white stones. From here you stand at the foot of the escarpment, looking towards the cliffs you'll be walking along.

The trail starts above the beach at the treeline and leads to the top of the escarpment where you can look down onto the water. In this area, the waters mimic the Carribean, with bright turquoise and deep blue hues. On several occasions, the trail leads you to rocky beaches before dipping back into the forest.

After Cave Point, the trail gets rockier with some scrambling. At Storm Haven, a wooden walkway leads to the rocky beach and limestone ledges. Listen to the waves. The water laps against the rocks at Storm Haven, a wonderful lullaby if you're camping overnight.

There are many lookouts along this trail, some that offer a bird's eye view on rock outcrops below, others that open to a wide rocky beach. When the trail takes you down to the beach on a logging road, it's the last time the trail comes down to the water. This is a difficult section to find your way out of. Stay along the rock ledges till you see a big arrow on your left. When you near an outcrop by the water, you'll find a big white arrow on one of the rock slabs pointing back up into the forest. The trail eventually meets up with the Horse Lake Trail which leads to head of trails in Cyprus Lake campground (follow the red blazes).

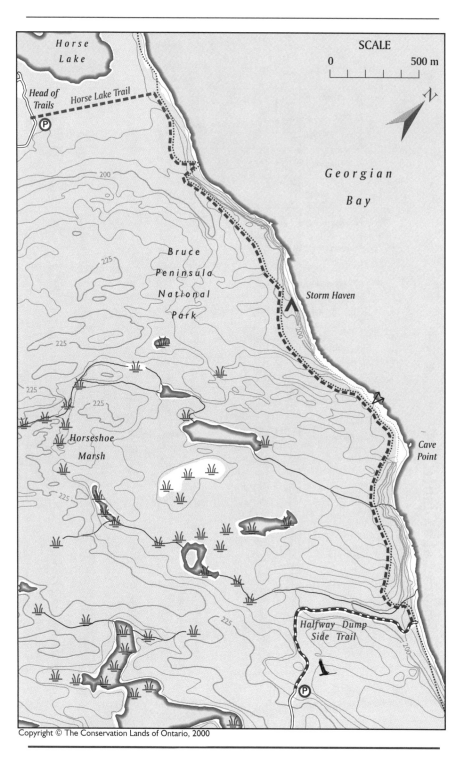

Horse
Lake

Head of
Trails

Horse Lake Trail

P

SCALE

0   500 m

N

Georgian

Bay

Bruce

Peninsula

National

Park

200

225

225

225

225

225

Storm Haven

Horseshoe
Marsh

Cave
Point

225

Halfway   Dump
Side Trail

200

P

Copyright © The Conservation Lands of Ontario, 2000

Trail Features at a Glance

	Cross Country Skiing	Viewing Area	Group Trail Bookings	Handicapped Access	Camping	Heritage Site	Interpretive/ Nature Centre	Special Events	Birding	Waterfall	Wetland	Niagara Escarpment
NIAGARA PENINSULA CONSERVATION AUTHORITY												
Hog Back Side Trail	•								•		•	•
Rockway Falls Side Trail		•	•						•	•	•	•
Beamer Trail	•			•				•	•			•
HAMILTON REGION CONSERVATION AUTHORITY												
Devil's Punch Bowl Trail	•	•							•			•
Rock Chapel Trail		•			•	•	•		•	•		•
Tiffany Falls Trail			•						•	•		•
Stairway to Spencer Gorge Trail		•	•						•	•		•
CONSERVATION HALTON												
Waterdown Trail	•	•				•			•	•	•	•
Nassagaweya Canyon Trail		•	•		•	•	•	•	•		•	•
Sixteen Mile Creek Trail	•	•		•		•			•	•	•	•

	Cross Country Skiing	Viewing Area	Group Trail Bookings	Handicapped Access	Camping	Heritage Site	Interpretive/ Nature Centre	Special Events	Birding	Waterfall	Wetland	Niagara Escarpment
CREDIT VALLEY CONSERVATION												
Walking Fern Side Trail	•								•		•	•
Terra Cotta to Silver Creek Trail	•	•			•				•		•	•
Trimble Trail		•	•		•	•		•	•		•	•
Meadow Side Trail	•	•				•			•	•	•	•
TORONTO AND REGION CONSERVATION AUTHORITY												
Albion Hills Trail	•				•		•	•	•		•	•
Palgrave Trail	•							•	•		•	•
Glen Haffy Trail	•				•				•		•	•
NOTTAWASAGA VALLEY CONSERVATION AUTHORITY												
Clifftop Side Trail	•	•							•		•	•
Primrose Loop	•	•							•			•
Keyhole Trail		•			•				•			•
Devil's Glen Provincial Park		•	•		•				•			•
Mad River Side Trail	•								•		•	•
Petun Conservation Area Trail	•				•				•		•	•

	Cross Country Skiing	Viewing Area	Group Trail Bookings	Handicapped Access	Camping	Heritage Site	Interpretive/Nature Centre	Special Events	Birding	Waterfall	Wetland	Niagara Escarpment
GREY SAUBLE CONSERVATION AUTHORITY												
Kolapore Uplands Trail	•	•			•				•		•	•
Walter's Falls Trail		•							•		•	•
The Glen Trail		•			•				•		•	•
Kemble Mountain Side Trail		•							•			•
Skinner's Bluff Trail	•	•				•			•			•
Jones Bluff Side Trail		•							•			•
BRUCE PENINSULA												
Gun Point Loop		•							•			•
Cave Point Trail		•			•				•			•

TRAIL INFORMATION

CONSERVATION AUTHORITY AND PARK CONTACTS

Niagara Peninsula Conservation Authority
2358 Centre Street, Allanburg, ON L0S 1A0
(905) 788-3135, fax (905) 788-1121,
e-mail: NPCA@niagara.com, website: www.conservation-niagara.on.ca

Hamilton Region Conservation Authority
838 Mineral Springs Rd., P.O. Box 7099, Ancaster, ON L9G 3L3
1-888-319-HRCA, (905) 648-4427, fax (905) 648-4622,
e-mail: nature@hamrca.on.ca, website: www.hamrca.on.ca

Conservation Halton
2596 Britannia Rd. W., R.R. #2 Milton, ON L9T 2X6
(905) 336-1158, fax (905) 336-7014,
e-mail: admin@hrca.on.ca, website: www.hrca.on.ca

Credit Valley Conservation
1255 Old Derry Road West, Meadowvale, ON L5N 6R4,
1-800-668-5557 (905) 670-1615, fax (905) 668-5557,
website: www.mississauga.com/conservation.html

Toronto and Region Conservation Authority
5 Shoreham Drive, Downsview, ON M3N 1S4,
(416) 661-6600, fax (905) 661-6898
e-mail: info@trca.on.ca, website: www.trca.on.ca

Nottawasaga Valley Conservation Authority
RR#1 Angus, ON L0M 1B0
(705) 424-1479, fax (705) 424-2115, e-mail: nvca@bconnex.net

Grey Sauble Conservation Authority
RR#4, Owen Sound, Ontario N4K 5N6
(519) 376-3076, fax (519) 371-0437, gsca@bmts.com

Bruce Peninsula National Park
P.O. Box 189, Tobermory, Ontario N0H 2R0
(519) 596-2233, fax (519) 596-2298,
e-mail: ont_bruce-peninsula@pch.gc.ca

THE CONSERVATION LANDS OF ONTARIO
400 Clyde Rd., P.O. Box 729
Cambridge, Ontario N1R 5W6
1-888-376-2212, fax (519) 621-4844
e-mail: conservationlands@grandriver.on.ca

NATIONAL AND PROVINCIAL TRAIL ASSOCIATIONS
*Refer to the Major Trail Links Section

REFERENCE BOOK INFORMATION

The Bruce Trail Reference by the Bruce Trail Association is highly recommended for its detailed description and topographical maps of the entire trail. The Guide has 40 five-colour fold-out topographical maps and comprehensive trail descriptions in a six-ring binder. It's available for $23.95 to Bruce Trail Members only, for $28.95 to non-members or from a range of $28.95 to $34.95 in bookstores and outdoor stores in Ontario.

The Bed and Breakfast Guide ($7.00) lists accommodation near or along the trail; *The Through-Hiker's Guide* ($6.00) includes valuable hiker's information from water availability to radio frequencies; and *The Environmental Hike Handbook* ($6.00) includes information about the geological sites along the Trail. Available in bookstores and from the Bruce Trail Association 905-529-6821, 1-800-665-4453, www.brucetrail.org.

Trails at the Tip o' the Bruce by Ross McLean (Friends of the Bruce District Parks Association, softcover, $7.95). Highly recommended for a detailed description of 13 Bruce Peninsula trails.

The Bruce Beckons by W. Sherwood Fox (University of Toronto Press, softcover, $17.95).

Guide to the Geology of the Niagara Escarpment by Dr. Walter M. Tovell (Niagara Escarpment Commission, softcover or binder format, $25.00). Call 905-877-5191 to order. Limited amount left and not reprinting this book.

The Beautiful Bruce Peninsula, a detailed road map published by the Tobermory Press (519) 596-2658.

Short Hills Provincial Park Trail Guide, by the Friends of Short Hills Park. A guide to history, geology and trails within the park.

Other Trail Guides by Katherine Jacob

Katherine Jacob has also published three other trail guides:

44 Country Trails by Katherine Jacob, a guide to trails of the Grand River, Halton Region, Hamilton Region, Long Point Region, and Niagara Peninsula Conservation Authorities, published by The Conservation Lands of Ontario.

Bruce Peninsula Trails by Katherine Jacob, a guide to trails of the Bruce Peninsula, Grey Sauble, Saugeen Valley and Maitland Valley regions.

Grand River Country Trails by Katherine Jacob, a guide to trails in the Brantford, Cambridge, Guelph, Kitchener and Waterloo region, published by *The Record*.

These three books are available through The Conservation Lands of Ontario 1-888-376-2212, and at many bookstores and outfitting stores.

To Help Preserve These Trails

You can help preserve any of the trails in this book that you have enjoyed. Just contact any of the following organizations to make a donation toward trail maintenance and preservation. It's always a good feeling to give something back.

THE BRUCE TRAIL ASSOCIATION
PO Box 857
Hamilton, Ontario L8N 3N9
905-529-6821, 1-800-665-4453, fax 905-529-6823
e-mail: info@brucetrail.org, www.brucetrail.org

Realizing the Dream by 2015 is a strategy to secure the trail in 15 years. For every step you donate ($25 for 1 footstep), 3 more steps are secured. Currently more than 50% of the Bruce Trail is not secured and the BTA is working together with the provincial government, major corporations, foundations and non-government partners to change this. Making this donation will preserve the Escarpment and our pathway through it.

NIAGARA PENINSULA CONSERVATION AUTHORITY
Niagara Peninsula Conservation, 2358 Centre Street, Allanburg, ON L0S 1A0
(905) 788-3135, fax (905) 788-1121, e-mail: NPCA@niagara.com,
website: www.conservation-niagara.on.ca

FRIENDS OF SHORT HILLS PROVINCIAL PARK
c/o Short Hills Provincial Park, P.O. Box 158, Dunnville, Ontario N1A 2X5

HAMILTON REGION CONSERVATION AUTHORITY
Conservation Foundation of the Hamilton Region, P.O. Box 7099, 838 Mineral Springs Road, Ancaster, Ontario L9G 3L3 (905) 525-2181 xt. 168,
fax (905) 648-4622, conservation@interlynx.net, http://conservation.interlynx.net

FRIENDS OF THE RED HILL VALLEY
68-151 Gateshead Crescent, Stoney Creek, Ontario L8G 3W1 (905) 381-0240.

CONSERVATION HALTON
Conservation Halton Foundation, 2596 Britannia Rd. W., R.R. #2 Milton,
ON L9T 2X6 (905) 336-1158 xt. 255, fax (905) 336-7014, e-mail: fund@hrca.on.ca

TORONTO AND REGION CONSERVATION AUTHORITY
Conservation Foundation of Greater Toronto, 5 Shoreham Drive, Downsview, ON M3N 1S4, (416) 661-6600 xt. 5207, fax (905) 661-6898 e-mail: info@trca.on.ca,
website: www.trca.on.ca

CREDIT VALLEY CONSERVATION
Credit Valley Conservation Foundation,1255 Old Derry Road West
Meadowvale, ON L5N 6R4, 1-800-668-5557 (905) 670-1615, fax (905) 668-5557,
website: www.mississauga.com/conservation.html

NOTTAWASAGA CONSERVATION AUTHORITY
Nottawasaga Valley Conservation Foundation, R.R. 1 Utopia, LOM 1TO.

GREY SAUBLE CONSERVATION AUTHORITY
Grey Sauble Conservation Foundation, RR#4, Owen Sound, Ontario N4K 5N6
(519) 376-3076, fax (519) 371-0437, gsca@bmts.com

BRUCE PENINSULA NATIONAL PARK
Friends of Bruce District Parks Association
(Fathom Five Park and the Flowerpot Island Lightstation)
PO Box 66, Tobermory, Ontario
N0H 2R0

FRIENDS OF CABOT HEAD
PO Box 233
Lion's Head, Ontario
N0H 1W0

You can also make a charitable donation to support The Conservation Lands of
Ontario. Projects you can support include: environmental restoration, future trail
guides, public information programs, etc.

THE CONSERVATION LANDS OF ONTARIO
400 Clyde Rd., P.O. Box 729, Cambridge, Ontario N1R 5W6
1-888-376-2212, fax (519) 621-4844
e-mail: conservationlands@grandriver.on.ca

OTHER ORGANIZATIONS THAT ACCEPT DONATIONS
Ontario Trails Council 1-877-668-7245
Box 462, Stn. D., Etobicoke, Ontario M9A 4X4

Niagara Escarpment Commission, 232 Guelph St., Georgetown, Ontario. L7G 4B1
(905) 877-5191, fax (905) 873-7452. Website: http://escarpment.org

Coalition on the Niagara Escarpment, 517 College Street, Suite 237,
Toronto, Ontario M6G 4A2 (416) 960-2008, fax (416) 960-0020,
e-mail: cone@interlog.com

Trip Planning

The following pages outline a few of the services, accommodations, and recreational opportunities available near trails featured in this book.

Ontario Tourism
1 Concord Gate
9th floor
Don Mills, Ontario
M3C 3N6
1-800-668-2746, French line: 800-268-3736, fax 416-443-6818
e-mail:info@travelinx.com, website: www.travelinx.com

Southern Ontario Tourism Organization
180 Greenwich St.
Brantford, Ont.
N3S 2X6
1-800-267-3399, fax 519-756-3231
e-mail: festival@niagara-midwest-ont.com, website: www.niagara-midwest-ont.com

The Bruce County Tourism Office
County of Bruce: Box 180
Southampton, Ontario
N0H 2L0
1-800-268-3838, fax (519) 797-2191, www.brucecounty.on.ca

Home to Home B&B
Bed & Breakfast Network
RR#4 Lion's Head, Ontario N0H 1W0
They offer a reserved room and luggage transfer for Bruce Trail hikes from Wiarton to Tobermory

Grey Bruce Tourism Association
RR#5 Owen Sound, Ontario N4K 5N7
(800) 265-3127, (519) 371-2071, fax (519) 371-5315, gbta@osiocom.net, www.visitontario.com

CAMPSITES

NIAGARA PENINSULA CONSERVATION AUTHORITY
Dressel's Jordan Valley Campground (905) 562-7816
45 serviced, 45 unserviced

HAMILTON REGION CONSERVATION AUTHORITY
Dundas Valley Conservation Area, Dundas (905) 627-1233
1 large group camping unserviced site
Group and Bruce Trail user camping only. No family camping.
Must call for reservation.
Copetown Holiday Park (close to Tiffany/Borer's Falls) (905) 648-3108
Confederation Park (close to Devil's Punchbowl)
(905) 578-1644, 50 serviced, 50 unserviced
Fifty Point Conservation Area and Marina (close to Devil's Punchbowl)
(905) 525-2187, 42 serviced sites, 5 unserviced sites

CONSERVATION HALTON
Kelso Conservation Area (905) 878-5011
15 unserviced group campsites

CREDIT VALLEY CONSERVATION
Terra Cotta Conservation Area
2 unserviced group campsites booked through 1-800-892-4646 or (519) 826-5315

TORONTO AND REGION CONSERVATION AUTHORITY
Glen Haffy Conservation Area (416) 661-6600
1 unserviced group campsite
Albion Hill Conservation Area (905) 880-0227
62 unserviced, 172 serviced

NOTTAWASAGA VALLEY CONSERVATION AUTHORITY
Nottawasaga Bluffs Conservation Area
1 unserviced group campsite, no pre-registration (first come first serve basis)

GREY SAUBLE CONSERVATION AUTHORITY CAMPSITES
None

BRUCE PENINSULA CAMPSITES

Cyprus Lake Campground, Tobermory (519) 596-2233
242 unserviced sites

Cape Croker, Cape Croker (519) 534-0571
Serviced sites, unserviced sites and seasonal sites

Backcountry sites are available at High Dump (on the Halfway Log Dump Trail) on a first come, first serve basis.

GRAND RIVER CONSERVATION AUTHORITY, (519) 621-2761

Eight campgrounds with 3,000 campsites, west of much of the Bruce Trail

PUBLIC SWIMMING BEACHES

NIAGARA PENINSULA CONSERVATION AUTHORITY
Lakeside Park
Long Beach
Sherkston Beach
Charles Daly Park
Nickel Beach

HAMILTON REGION CONSERVATION AUTHORITY
Valen's Conservation Area
Christie Conservation Area

CONSERVATION HALTON
Kelso Conservation Area

CREDIT VALLEY CONSERVATION
Island Lake Conservation Area

TORONTO AND REGION CONSERVATION AUTHORITY
Albion Hills Conservation Area

NOTTAWASAGA CONSERVATION AUTHORITY
Wasaga Beach
New Lowell Conservation Area

GREY SAUBLE CONSERVATION AUTHORITY
Southampton
Red Bay
Christie Beach
Kelso Beach

CANOE AND KAYAK ROUTES

NIAGARA PENINSULA CONSERVATION AUTHORITY

The Welland River flows placidly along its flat gradient from Port Davidson to Welland. The 40 km (25 mile) route meanders through agricultural land and a developed stretch of recreational areas such as campsites, golf courses and private cottages.

To explore this section of the river, camp at Chippawa Creek Conservation Area, located three kilometres (two miles) west of the village of Wellandport. The Conservation Area has two earth-filled dams constructed in an old meander of the river to create a 14 hectare (35 acre) reservoir named Dils lake. Non-power motorboats and canoes are permitted on the lake and a launching ramp is provided for boats entering the river.

From this site, paddle upstream for approximately four miles before reaching the Port Davidson Weir. The weir is easily portaged and beyond this point lie ten kilometres (six miles) of open stream. The Oswego Creek, the Welland's main tributary, can also be explored from this location with open water for at least three kilometres (two miles). Another access point to the river is the E.C. Brown Conservation Area.

NOTTAWASAGA CONSERVATION AUTHORITY

The Nottawasaga River Canoe Route takes paddlers through the Internationally Recognized Minnesing Swamp, filled with Carolinian woodlands, numerous waterfowl and songbirds. The route from Angus to Edenvale is 20 kilometres (12.4 miles) long and begins at the NVCA main office on County Rd. 90. The starting point is signed. Small logjams are enroute with a large one at the confluence of the Nottawasaga River and the Willow Creek.

The Willow Creek route starts at the Minnesing Swamp Conservation Area on George Johnston Rd. (County Rd. 28) 1.6 kilometres (one mile) south of the village of Minnesing. This route winds through the open meadows, silver maple forests and eventually joins with the Nottawasaga River and ends at Edenvale. Spring is the best time for waterfowl sightings. Beware of low water in the summer, some poling may be required periodically.

GREY SAUBLE CONSERVATION AUTHORITY

The 20 kilometre (12 mile) Beaver River canoe route offers views of the Niagara Escarpment, surrounding farmland, and silver maple woodlands. It begins at the access located on Grey County Road 13, approximately 2 kilometres (1.3 miles) north east of Kimberly. Short portages may be required to bypass logjams.

The 18 kilometre (11 mile) Rankin River canoe route winds through shallow, weedy lakes bordered by woodlands and marsh, past a control dam and two short sections of rapids. The rapids must be lined or portaged in times of low water.

BRUCE PENINSULA

There are various kayaking routes along the Lake Huron shoreline with inlets, coves and islands to explore. For an overnight kayaking trip, there are six campsites on Flowerpot Island available on a first come, first serve basis. Be aware that Lake Huron's waters are difficult to predict. During stormy days, high winds, strong waves and the rocky shoreline can be very dangerous. Before taking an extended trip, check for detailed weather reports.

INDEX

ALPHABETICAL TRAILS LISTING

TRAIL LISTING BY COMMUNITY

PHOTO CREDITS

KATHERINE JACOB
Hilton Falls, p. 8
Trilliums, p. 10
Fox Cubs, p. 51
Hilton Falls, p. 58
Halfway Log Dump, p. 75

ROB STIMPSON
Kelso, Front Cover
Rattlesnake Point, p. 19
Rattlesnake Point, p. 40
Wild Ginger, p. 41
Burns Conservation Area, p. 50
Hilton Falls, p. 59
Rattlesnake Point, p. 74

About the Author

Since she was a child, writer and photographer Katherine Jacob has loved nature. Her writing focuses on the outdoors and has appeared in a variety of publications, from *Equinox* and *Canadian Wildlife* to *The Toronto Star* and *The Globe and Mail*. Katherine is the author of three other Canadian bestselling books, *44 Country Trails, Bruce Peninsula Trails* and *Grand River Country Trails*. She also writes two hiking columns: "Nature Walks" for *The Globe and Mail* and "Trail Markers" for *The Record*.

OTHER BOOKS BY KATHERINE JACOB